10u

2/14/54

Pete:

I derive a great deal of secret pride in knowing that this may be shelved somewhere near the finest collection of Henty in existence.

Happy Valentine's...

CHRISTOPHER MORLEY

From the painting of Joseph Hinsch

A Bibliography of
CHRISTOPHER MORLEY

by

Guy R. Lyle

and

H. Tatnall Brown, Jr.

The Scarecrow Press
Washington 7, D.C.
1952

PREFACE

For several reasons a preface is necessary to this book. Especially, because I wish to express my indebtedness to two persons, but for whom I should not have set myself to this exacting though agreeable task.

In the autumn of 1935, Doubleday, Doran & Co. published the valuable bibliography of Christopher Morley by the late Dr. Alfred P. Lee. Although my interest in collecting Morleyana preceded this work by many years, it was not until I owned a copy of Lee's valuable work that I started making bibliographical notes of Morley's writings. Twelve years later, when I was putting together the notes out of which the present book has grown, I learned through Mr. Ben Abramson of the Argus Book Shop that Dr. Lee had prepared a revision of his bibliography before his death in 1940 and through the courtesy of Mr. Abramson I was given an opportunity to examine these notes. To these two persons, therefore, the late Dr. Alfred P. Lee, to whom I should like to dedicate this volume as a tribute to a distinguished bibliographer, and to Mr. Abramson, I am happy to express my deep appreciation and indebtedness.

The Lee bibliography describes the first printings in the English language of the writings of Christopher Morley down through 1934, books to which Morley made contributions, ephemeral publications, and books by other writers containing comment on Morley's work. The present volume continues the bibliographical listing for each of these four sections down through 1951, and records, in addition, the periodical articles by and about Morley from the beginning in 1908. Full description is given for first editions with mention of any subsequent edition in which extensive alteration and revision may be found. Reprints of popular, inexpensive editions are excluded unless they contain new material, such as a new preface. In order to minimize the inconvenience of using two books, all titles in the Lee volume are listed by title and date in the present work with page references to where the full collations may be found in Lee. In some cases these title listings may be followed by a note correcting the original collation in Lee; in other instances early titles omitted from Lee have been incorporated into their proper chronological place with full collations. With few exceptions these corrections and additions to the earlier work were taken from the notes left by Dr. Lee.

The arrangement of titles in the present work is chronological by date of publication for all writings except the section entitled "Ephemeral Publications" which is arranged alphabetically by title. In many cases it was impossible to determine the date of these minor contributions. A full description is given of first editions of books and the more important pamphlets. An exception to the chronological arrangement in this section is made for books of the same title. Later editions with substantial changes follow the first edition. Shorter collations are given for contributions by Morley to other books and for books which contain material about Morley.

A list of contributions to periodicals in the case of a writer who does much miscellaneous work can never be complete. Christopher Morley has suggested that "this subaltern matter" be excluded and that a separate mimeographed list be supplied, if desired, to "libraries, fellow-bibliographers, or hyperthyroid collectors." The compilers appreciate the intent of this suggestion but prefer to leave the problem of selection to the user of the bibliography. They believe that an author bibliography should be made as complete as possible. Anyone who wants to pay his way is at liberty to wander about, to select the important, to reject the ephemeral, or to make trouble in other ways. Even so, it is recognized that the periodical section of the bibliography is incomplete. Book reviews are not included.

I wish to express here my appreciation of the interest and assistance of many who have contributed to make this volume possible. I am indebted to Mr. Morley for permission to compile the bibliography, and for friendly advice and encouragement throughout the work. My collaborator, H. Tatnall Brown, Jr., read the manuscript and made many helpful corrections and suggestions. For many services I am indebted to the reference staff of the Louisiana State University Library, Miss Ruth Walling, Chief Reference Librarian, and to my friends and colleagues in other libraries. To all of them, I express my deepest appreciation.

G.R.L.

July 3, 1952

CHRONOLOGICAL TABLE

1890   Christopher Darlington Morley born, in Haverford, Penn., May 5. His father, a distinguished mathematician, was professor of mathematics at Haverford, later at Johns Hopkins University. His mother was a musician.

1910   Graduated from Haverford College.

1910-13 Rhodes scholar at New College, Oxford. Two brothers were also Rhodes scholars.

1912   The Eighth Sin, Morley's first book of poems, was published by the famous English bookseller B. H. Blackwell.

1913-17 Member of the editorial staff of Doubleday, Page and Company.

1914   Married Helen Booth Fairchild; four children.

1917   Parnassus on Wheels, first novel.

1917-18 By his own words one of "the little group of wilful men who edit the Ladies' Home Journal."

1918-20 Editorial contributor and columnist for Philadelphia Evening Public Ledger.

1920-23 Wrote The Bowling Green column in the New York Evening Post.

1924-38 Contributing editor and columnist (The Bowling Green, Trade Winds) for the Saturday Review of Literature.

1928   Member of the editorial board of the Book-Of-The-Month Club from its inception.
With Cleon Throckmorton, founded in Hoboken, N.J., a theater where old melodramas, After Dark and The Black Crook, were successfully revived.

1930   Appointed first fellow Rosenbach Fellowship in Bibliography, University of Pennsylvania. His lectures, given in 1931,

were published under title <u>Ex</u> <u>Libris</u>
<u>Carissimis</u> (1932).

1933   Honorary degree of D.Litt. Haverford
College.

1935   Address Mark Twain Commemoration,
delivered at Columbia University,
October 31.

1937   Editor-in-chief Bartlett's <u>Familiar</u> <u>Quo-</u>
<u>tations</u>, eleventh edition.
Annual Hopwood address, delivered University of Michigan, June 2. "A successor to Mark Twain."

1938   William L. Honnold Foundation lecturer
at Knox College, Illinois.

1939   Visiting lecturer at Adelphi College, N.Y.;
again in 1940.

1944   Honorary degree LL.D. Adelphi College,
N.Y.

1947   <u>Notes</u> <u>on</u> <u>an</u> <u>Island</u>, memoranda of a two
months' visit to post-war England, his
first return in seventeen years.

1949   <u>The</u> <u>Man</u> <u>Who</u> <u>Made</u> <u>Friends</u> <u>With</u> <u>Himself</u>,
the novel that he felt should be the climax
of this small bibliographical work.

CONTENTS

I. BOOKS AND PAMPHLETS

Separates appearing in the Lee bibliography are listed here by title only, followed by a page reference to where the full collation in Lee may be found and by the date of the title. In a few instances these title listings are followed by a note correcting or adding something to the original collations in Lee. Full collations, of course, are given for separates appearing after the publication of Lee (1935) as well as for a few earlier titles which did not appear in Lee.

THE EIGHTH SIN (3-4)
1912

THE BOOKSELLER'S BLUE BOOK (5)
1914

THE BOOKSELLER'S BLUE BOOK (6)
1914-15

MAKING BOOKS AND MAGAZINES (7-8)
1916
Lee p. 7, line 11: 16mo should read 18mo.

PARNASSUS ON WHEELS (9-10)
1917

SONGS FOR A LITTLE HOUSE (11-12)
1917

SHANDYGAFF (13-14)
1918

THE ROCKING HORSE (15-16)
1919

THE HAUNTED BOOKSHOP (17-19)
1919

IN THE SWEET DRY AND DRY (20-21)
1919

MINCE PIE (22-23)
1919

CHRISTOPHER MORLEY ON THE AMENITIES
OF BOOK-COLLECTING (24)
1919

KATHLEEN (25-26)
1920

GENTLES, ATTEND! (27)
1920

Lee p. 27, line 16: Delete word "copies." Following word "today," insert: What appear to be the earliest copies of this broadside contain many typographical errors, most of which received correction before the main run was made. A list of these errors (the ones corrected in later impressions) follows: (The line numbers refer to those of the broadside.)

Line   9 - Change "one apple" to "I apply."
  "   10 - Insert word "one" before SIDNEY.
  "   21 - Insert spaces before and after word "but."
  "   22 - Transfer first two letters in word "ahste."
  "   39 - Remove letter "s" from word "times."
  "   40 - Insert letter "e" in word "Amrican."
  "   51 - Make third word "fair" instead of "pair."
  "   57 - Insert spaces before and after word "as."
  "   60 - Insert space between words "he" and "does."
  "   63 - Change "whim" to "whom."
  "   71 - Change word "that" to "the."
  "   77 - Transfer space and letter "f" in "of whom."

"   79 - Change word "aharms" to
        "charms."
"   90 - Make QUIZ EDITOR one word:
        QUIZEDITOR.
"   92 - Insert space between words "of" and
        "bookishness."
"   98 - Insert space after colon.
" 113 - Change God to Cod.
" 122 - Change "swett" to "sweet."
" 126 - Transfer letters "u" and "l" in
        word "Culbs."
" 136 - Change MALEY to HALEY.
Retain as separate paragraph: The manuscript
is in the Huntington Library.

TRAVELS IN PHILADELPHIA (28-29)
        1920

TRAVELS IN PHILADELPHIA
New Edition
        1937
Christopher Morley / [double rule] / Travels In /
Philadelphia / With Illustrations By / Herbert
Pullinger / And / Frank H. Taylor / [eleven-line
quotation] / Charles Godfrey Leland, 1893 / Phil-
adelphia & New York / J. B. Lippincott Company /
London
COLLATION: 12mo. Pp. [i-x]-xi-xiii-[xiv]-xv-
[xviii]+ 7*-264, consisting of p. [i] fly title
Travels / In / Philadelphia / A New Edition with /
Additional Illustrations; verso blank; frontispiece
not included in the pagination has recto blank,
verso drawing entitled Rooftops; p. [iii] title as
above; verso Copyright, 1920, By / David McKay
Company / Copyright, 1937, By / J. B. Lippincott
Company / Made In The / United States Of /
America; p. [v] Affectionately Dedicated To / Bart
Haley / (The Soothsayer) / Jimmy Craven / (The
Epicure) / Roy Helton / (The Mountaineer) / My
Genial Tutors In The Delicate Art / Of Living In

Philadelphia; verso blank; pp. [vii-viii] Postscript, For This New Edition, signed A. Edward Newton / "Oak Knoll" / Daylesford, Pa. / April 18, 1937; p. [ix] Author's Note; verso blank; pp. xi-xiii Introduction, signed A. Edward Newton / Daylesford, Pa. / January 20, 1920; p. [xiv] blank; pp. xv-xvi Contents; p. [xvii] Illustrations; verso blank; pp. 7-264 text. There are full half-tone illustrations pp. [iii] frontispiece, 10, 14, 42, 50, 82, 130, 142, 162, 212, 228, 240, and 242, which are not included in the pagination.

*No leaves to allow for paging [1-6].

Wove paper, watermarked American / Eggshell Text. Top and bottom edges trimmed, others untrimmed. Top edges stained blue. Bound in blue cloth with tan linen backbone. Front, in gold, reads Travels In Philadelphia / By Christopher Morley. Blue cloth label on backbone reads, in gold, [three rules] / [dotted lines] / Travels / In / Philadelphia / [dotted circle] / Christopher / Morley / [dotted circle] / Lippincott / [dotted line] / [three rules]

The jacket is white with illustration in tan decorative panel by Herbert Pullinger. Front reads, in red, Travels / In / Philadelphia / Christopher Morley. Same design and lettering on small scale is repeated on the backstrip, and at bottom is added, in red, Lippincott. Back has a list of books by Morley published by Lippincott. Front flap carries a note about this new edition of the "Travels"; back flap carries advertisement of "Hasta La Vista."
Contains a new postscript by A. Edward Newton and nine new illustrations by Herbert Pullinger. Issued December 6, 1937 with a first printing of 1000 copies.

HIDE AND SEEK (30-31)
1920

PIPEFULS (32-33)
1920

THE CHRISTMAS TOBACCO (34)
1920

TALES FROM A ROLLTOP DESK (35-36)
1921

PLUM PUDDING (37-38)
1921

MODERN ESSAYS (39-40)
1921
Lee p. 39, line 6: Insert after word "Company": /
1921
Lee p. 40: Add to final paragraph: Page 54, Line
25: Third word reads "affroat" instead of
"afloat." This error was not corrected in the
first reprinting.

MODERN ESSAYS FOR SCHOOLS (41-42)
1922
Lee p. 42: Add to first paragraph: Page 54, Line
25: The third word reads "affroat" instead of
"afloat." This error was not corrected in the
first reprinting.

MODERN ESSAYS (SECOND SERIES) (43-44)
1924

CHIMNEYSMOKE (45-46)
1921

A CHRISTMAS CARD TO WOODROW WILSON (47)
1921

IN RE LOGAN PEARSALL SMITH (48)
[1921]

THURSDAY EVENING (49-50)
1922

THE STORY OF GINGER CUBES (51)
1922

TRANSLATIONS FROM THE CHINESE (52-53)
1922

TRANSLATIONS FROM THE CHINESE (54-55)
1927

WHERE THE BLUE BEGINS (56-58)
1922

WHERE THE BLUE BEGINS (59-60)
[1924]
Large Paper Edition
Lee p. 60: Add to third paragraph: American
Large-Paper Edition: Page 150, Line 2: Change
"gloves" to "globes." Same title, English Large-
Paper Edition, same correction. The English
book is one-quarter inch less in height than the
American book, and the top edges are stained deep
blue. The American Large-Paper Edition,
Limited, Signed, also contains this error, but the
English Large-Paper Edition, Limited, Signed,
has received correction.

WHERE THE BLUE BEGINS (61-62)
[1924]
Large-Paper Edition, Limited, Signed

WHERE THE BLUE BEGINS: A DIVINE
COMEDY (63-64)
1925

THE POWDER OF SYMPATHY (65-66)
1923
Lee p. 66: Add to final paragraph: A later binding,
but of the first edition sheets, has boards of
deeper orange and a black backbone.

INWARD HO! (67-68)
1923

PARSONS' PLEASURE (69-70)
1923

CONRAD AND THE REPORTERS (71-72)
1923

AN APOLOGY FOR BOCCACCIO (73-74)
1923

AN APOLOGY FOR BOCCACCIO (75)
1923
Large-Paper Issue of Four Copies

CONCERNING A PAINTING
1924
Concerning A Painting / Of Robert Louis Stevenson / By Will H. Low / Printed for private circu-
lation. / Bronx Valley Press / Bronxville, N. Y.
1924
COLLATION: 12mo. Pp. [1-2]-3-7-[8]-9-17-[18],
consisting of p. [1] title as above; verso blank, but
carrying a tipped-in half-tone illustration, with
line at lower right reading Copyright by Will H.
Low; pp. 3-7 text, captioned Notes On A Painting /
Reprinted from the New York Evening Post / October 18th, 1923, text opening with four-line
initial, closing with signature Christopher Morley;
p. [8] blank, but carrying a tipped-in half-tone
illustration; pp. 9-11 text, captioned Forest
Notes: / First printed in the Cornhill Magazine,
May 1876, / and now published in the Thistle

Edition of Stevenson's / works, vol. **XXII**, text
opening with four-line initial, closing with signature Robert Louis Stevenson and tailpiece;
pp. 12-17 text, captioned A Few Observations /
Principally Technical, by the Painter, closing with
signature Will H. Low.; p. [18] blank. One fly
leaf at back.

Laid paper, watermarked Covenant / Book. Top
and bottom edges trimmed, front edges untrimmed.
Bound in heavy blue wrappers, front reading, in
dark blue, Concerning A Painting / Of Robert
Louis Stevenson / 1875-1923. Stitched with blue
silk cord.
No jacket.

OUTWARD BOUND (76-77)
    1924

THE BOWLING GREEN (78-79)
    1924

PANDORA LIFTS THE LID (80-81)
    1924

ONE ACT PLAYS (82-83)
    1924

RELIGIO JOURNALISTICI (84-85)
    1924

A BOOKSELLER'S BREVIARY (86-87)
    [1924]

FORTY-FOUR ESSAYS (88-89)
    1925

REHEARSAL (90)
    1925

HOSTAGES TO FORTUNE (91-92)
1925

TWO FABLES (93-94)
1925
Lee p. 94: Insert as final paragraph: Page 50,
Line 19: Second "i" is missing in word
"privileged."

A GOLDEN STRING (95)
1925

THUNDER ON THE LEFT (96-98)
1925
Lee p. 97: Insert semicolon instead of comma at
end of Line 16. Continue, as Line 17: at West
Falmouth, Mass., the week beginning July 21,
1930, under the sponsorship of the University
Players; and then continue with Line 17 as originally printed. Same page, Line 30: word "cloth"
should read "boards."

TWO PREFACES BY WALT WHITMAN (99-100)
1926

THE ROMANY STAIN (101-102)
1926

THE ROMANY STAIN (103-104)
1926
Large-Paper Limited Edition, Signed

GOOD THEATRE (105-106)
1926

PAUMANOK (107-108)
1926

THE ARROW (109-110)
1927

PLEASED TO MEET YOU (111-112)
1927
Lee p. 112, line 7: Insert as paragraph: "Pleased to Meet You" and "The Arrow" were also issued together in a single board case, both marked First Edition. Line 12: After word "title" insert: opening quotation marks before word "The" and delete same before word "Arrow."

THE CENTURY (113)
1927

HAVERFORD COLLECTED EDITION (114-119)
1927

I KNOW A SECRET (120-121)
1927

EPIGRAMS IN A CELLAR (122)
1927

THE CASE OF BOUCK WHITE (123-124)
1927

MY ONE CONTRIBUTION TO SEVENTEENTH CENTURY SCHOLARSHIP (125)
1927

THE TREE THAT DIDN'T GET TRIMMED (126)
1927

TOULEMONDE (127-128)
1928

ESSAYS (129-130)
1928

A LETTER TO LEONORA (131)
1928

A LETTER TO LEONORA (132)
1928
Large-Paper Edition, Limited, Signed

THE OLD RIALTO THEATRE (133)
[1928]

REALLY, MY DEAR. . . (134)
1928

A RIDE IN THE CAB OF THE TWENTIETH
CENTURY LIMITED (135-136)
1928

OFF THE DEEP END (137-138)
1928

THE WORST CHRISTMAS STORY (139-140)
1928

THE HOUSE OF DOONER (141)
1928

SEACOAST OF BOHEMIA (142-143)
1929

SEACOAST OF BOHEMIA (144)
1929
Limited Edition

MR. HUTAF SEES HOBOKEN IN AQUILINE
PERSPECTIVE (145)
1929

PASSPORT, HOBOKEN FREE STATE (146-147)
1929

"IN MODERN DRESS" (148)
1929

13

TRANSYLVANIA (149-150)
1929

POEMS (151-152)
1929

THE PALETTE KNIFE (153-154)
1929

A PROLOGUE FOR THE OLD RIALTO THEATRE,
HOBOKEN (155)
[1929]

BORN IN A BEER GARDEN (156-158)
1930

BORN IN A BEER GARDEN (159)
1930
Limited Edition, Signed

SUN CURED (160)
1930

THE FOUNDRY (161)
1930

THE BLUE AND THE GRAY (162-163)
1930
Limited Edition, Signed

THE BLUE AND THE GRAY (164)
1930
Trade Edition

APOLOGIA PRO SUA PREOCCUPATIONE
(165-166)
1930

ON THE NOSE (167)
1930

A BOOK OF DAYS (168-169)
1930
Lee p. 169: Insert in paragraph ending ". . . first printing of 5000 copies.": At least four colors of cloth were used in binding this book, but the grayish green appears to have been the first placed on sale.

RUDOLPH AND AMINA (170-171)
1930

THE GOLDFISH UNDER THE ICE (172)
1929

THE GOLDFISH UNDER THE ICE (173-174)
1932
American Edition

"WHEN WE SPEAK OF A TENTH=" (175)
1931

JOHN MISTLETOE (176-177)
1931

ON VISITING BOOKSHOPS (178)
1931

CHRISTOPHER MORLEY REVIEWS ONE DAY'S NEWS IN THE NEW YORK TIMES (179)
1931

CHRISTOPHER MORLEY AGAIN REVIEWS ONE DAY'S NEWS IN . . . THE NEW YORK TIMES
1933
Christopher Morley / Again Reviews One / Day's News in . . . The New York Times
COLLATION: 18mo. Pp. [1-2]-3-14-[15-16], consisting of p. [1] title as above; verso, center, The New York Times / Advertising Department Series / Number 62; bottom, Reprinted by

courtesy of / Mr. Christopher Morley / and The
Saturday Review of / Literature from its issue
of / July 29, 1933; pp. 3-[15] text, signed
Christopher Morley; p. [16] The New York
Times / "All the News That's Fit to Print."
The cover, included in the pagination, is of coated
blue paper, with printing thereon in bronze-black.

DON'T OPEN UNTIL CHRISTMAS (180-181)
    1931

NOTES ON BERMUDA (182-183)
    1931

BLYTHE MOUNTAIN, VERMONT (184-185)
    1931

SWISS FAMILY MANHATTAN (186-187)
    1932

EX LIBRIS CARISSIMIS (188-189)
    1932
Lee p. 189: Add at end of second paragraph the
following note: Page 40, Line 15: The word
"Papers" should read "Life." Page 46, Lines
14-17 contain the words "by remembering" in
duplicate. Same page, Line 18: The word "ask"
should read "task."

MAX AND MORITZ (190-191)
    1932

HUMAN BEING (192-193)
    1932

MANDARIN IN MANHATTAN (194-195)
    1933

FIFTH AVENUE BUS (196-197)
    1933

SHAKESPEARE AND HAWAII (198-199)
1933

INTERNAL REVENUE (200-201)
1933

"EFFENDI" (202)
1934

HASTA LA VISTA (203-204)
1935

OLD LOOPY (205)
1935
Lee p. 205, add to last paragraph: A de luxe edition of ten copies bound in three-quarters morocco, and one of five copies in full morocco, were issued November 30, 1935. All copies had the printed name on the title page pen-deleted and signed instead in manuscript by the author. The binding was done by Leonard Mounteney of the Cuneo Press.

OLD LOOPY
Second Edition
1937
Old / Loopy / A Love Letter / For Chicago / By Christopher Morley / Photographs by Guy Eder- heimer, Jr. / [ornament, in red] / The Argus Book Shop, Inc. / Chicago - 1937
COLLATION: 8vo. Pp. [1-11]-12-21-[22-44], con- sisting of pp. [1-2] fly leaf included in pagination; p. [3] fly title Old / Loopy; verso blank; p. [5] cap- tion reading—queer, double note of the police whistles . . . . mocking, impu- / dent, ribald call . . . .; verso half tone; p. [7] title as above, the whole surrounded by a rule border in red and the top border showing sketch of skyline; verso Copyright 1937, By the Argus Book Shop / Old Loopy, in its original form, was first printed in

the Saturday Review / Of Literature on December
8, 1934. / Second Edition / Printed In The U.S.A.;
p. [9] Chicago / By Christopher Morley, a poem
consisting of fourteen lines; verso blank; pp. [11]-
21 half title Old / Loopy / By Christopher Morley,
followed by text opening with initial in red; p. [22]
blank; p. [23] second fly title Old Loopy / Illustrations; verso legend to photograph facing, on p. [25];
pp. [26-45] legends and photographs with same
treatment printed on buff calendared paper; p. [42]
blank; p. [43] Old Loopy / This Edition is Limited
to Seven / Hundred and seventy-five copies. / Designed By Rex Cleveland. / Typography and
Presswork By / The Falcon Press, Chicago,
U.S.A. / Completed In September, 1937. One blank
leaf at front, one at back.

Fancy wove paper, unwatermarked. All edges
trimmed. Bound in cream cloth. Lettering on
front, in three-quarter box in red, reads Old
Loopy / By Christopher Morley / Photographs by
Guy Ederheimer, Jr.

Buff jacket, design and lettering same as front
cover.
    Contains a new poem p. [9], not in the first edi-
    tion (Lee p. 205), entitled "Chicago." The
    format is quite different from the first edition.

BR'S SECRET PASSION (206)
            1935

A CHRISTMAS SALUTE
            1935
[ornament] / A Christmas / Salute / By /
Christopher / Morley / [ornament] / Philip C.
Duschnes . New York / 1935
COLLATION: La. 8vo. Twelve unnumbered pages,
consisting of p. [1] title as above, ornaments and
the line Salute printed in red, the whole surrounded

18

by a border wreath in green; verso Copyright 1935
Christopher Morley / First Edition; pp. [3-9] text
printed within borders similar to those on the title
page and opening with fancy initial in red; p. [10]
blank; p. [11] Three hundred copies of this booklet
have / been printed in December nineteen thirty- /
five for the friends of Philip C. Duschnes. /
Walpole Printing Office, Mt. Vernon, N.Y.; verso
blank. One blank leaf at front, one at back.

Cream wove paper, unwatermarked. All edges untrimmed. Bound in fancy cream wrappers. Front
cover in box reads A Christmas Salute /
Christopher Morley, the type and outside rule in
red, fancy type rule in green. Stitched with silk
cord.
 300 copies were printed at the Walpole Printing
 Office, December, 1935. With the exception of a
 portion of the final paragraph, the contents were
 originally printed in the "New York Evening
 Post," December 23, 1922.

"RARE" BOOKS
   1935
"Rare" Books / An Essay / by / Christopher /
Morley / [ornament] / New York / The Press of
the Booklet / 1935
COLLATION: 12mo. Pp. [i-ii]-1-9-[10], consisting
of p. [i] title as above; verso With grateful acknowledgment to Christopher / Morley and the
New York Evening Post / for permission to reprint this essay.; pp. 1-9 text; p. [10] Seventy-
five copies have been printed in / hand-set Bern-
hard type on antique / wove paper for the friends
of / William J. McElwee. / This is number
Cream wove paper, watermarked Strathmore Wayside Text. U.S.A. Bound in laid yellow wrappers,
front cover reading, in brown, "Rare" Books /
By / Christopher / Morley. Stitched with silk
cord.

First printed in the New York Evening Post, "Literary Review," January 20, 1923.

RUBAIYAT OF ACCOUNT OVERDUE
1935

Rubaiyat / of / Account Overdue / [ornament] / by / Christopher Morley / [ornament] / Gotham Book Mart / Fifty-one West Forty-seventh / New York, New York / M'C'M'X'X'X'V
COLLATION: La. 8vo. French fold, eight unnumbered pages, consisting of p. [1] title as above, in ornamental type border; pp. [2-3] blank; pp. [4-5] poem of five stanzas, ornaments between, closing Signed _____ / April 1935 _____ / Reserved for _____, both pages in ornamental type border; pp. [6-7] blank / p. [8][sketch] / Rubaiyat of Account Overdue, by / Christopher Morley, Written for / Frances Steloff, has been printed / in this Limited Edition of 350 copies / from Inkunabula Type, imported / from Italy. It was set by hand, and / the type has been distributed. / Designed and Printed by Lew Ney. / This Copy / is / Number / [ornament], the last four lines between brackets, with ornamental type border surrounding the page.

No covers.
Issued at same time was a broadside, 500 copies, printed on fancy wove paper 14" x 7½".
The poem was first printed in the "Saturday Review of Literature," April 20, 1935.

THE APOLOGIA OF THE AMPERSAND
1936

[Sketch in gray-blue, hand reaching for Ampersand, double rule of light blue beneath] / The Apologia of the Ampersand / Christopher Morley
COLLATION: 16mo. Pp. [1-8], consisting of p. [1] title as above; verso blank; pp. [3-7], cuts similar to that on title page, with four lines of a

20

poem, in italic, beneath each sketch; p. [8] similar
cut and rule, lines beneath reading Designed And
Printed By / The Powgen Press / With Linoleum
Cuts By / Chas. McCurdy.

Laid paper, no watermark. No covers.
   Appeared first as a signature in "Diggings
   From Many Ampersandhogs," (q.v.).

CHRISTOPHER MORLEY'S BRIEFCASE
       1935
Christopher / Morley's / Briefcase / [ornamental
design containing insignia of Three-Hours-for-
Lunch Club, below which appears 25¢ in relief] /
"The Way to Spread a Work is To > > >
COLLATION: 12mo. Pp. 1-64 consisting of ornamental rule, half-title Morley's Briefcase, single
rule, followed by title of first essay Dowager Of
The Sea, then text. The title, above, appears in
red on the front cover which is of heavy buff
wrappers, carries over to the inside and finishes
the quotation above, sell it at a low price."—Dr.
Johnson, quoted by Boswell, 1773. The inside
front cover carries a Partial Contents, publisher's
and copyright notices. The back inside cover has
advertisement of the S.R.L.; back cover advertisement of Morley's books.

Wove paper, no watermark. All edges trimmed.
No jacket.
   The copyright notice states that most of the
   material is reprinted from the author's contributions to the "Saturday Review of Literature." The book was published by J. B. Lippincott Company, Philadelphia, December 4, 1936,
   in an edition of 10,000 copies, of which 1000
   were later bound in cloth. Page 64 of the first
   printing reads PLAza 3-0403 which is corrected
   in later printings of this edition to PLaza
   3-0403.

On December 29, 1936, Lippincott issued an
edition carrying a title page, inserted in place
of the original page 1, and reading:
[ornamental rule] / Christopher Morley's /
Briefcase / [ornamental rule] / [publisher's
device] / J. B. Lippincott Company / Philadelphia & London; verso Copyright 1936 by
Christopher Morley / Printed in the United
States of America; p. [iii] Partial Contents,
followed by full page of text; verso blank.
This edition is bound in gray cloth, the front
reading in red Christopher / Morley's /
Briefcase. The jacket is of heavy buff paper
with all printing in red. 1000 copies of this
edition were published. The telephone number
PLAza 3-0403 appears as in first printing
in copies examined.

EX LIBRIS
          1936
Ex Libris / [sketch in brown] / A small Anthology,
printed and bound / (and sold) at the First National
Book / Fair sponsored by the New York Times /
and the National Association of Book / Publishers.
Compiled at their request by / Christopher
Morley / [ornamental line] / New York City:
November / 1936
COLLATION: 12mo. Fifty-four unnumbered
pages, consisting of p. [1] fly title [ornament] /
Ex Libris / [ornament] / Compiled by Christopher
Morley / ["The most important autograph / in a
book, is Your Own"]; verso blank; p. [3] title as
above with design of a cherub holding an open book
and ornamental line in brown; verso Individual
items reprinted herein, where still under / copyright, are subject to their original ownership. /
The collection as a whole is copyright Mcmxxxvi /
by Christopher Morley; p. [5] Note, followed by ten

22

lines on the typography, design, and publication of
the book; verso blank; pp. [7-8] introductory note
by Christopher Morley, dated October, 1936;
p. [9] second fly title [ornament] / Ex Libris /
[ornament] / Compiled by Christopher Morley;
verso blank; pp. [11-45] text; p. [46] blank; pp.
[47-52] Identifications; p. [53] About the Making of
this Book, followed by seventeen lines; verso
blank. One blank leaf at front, four at back.

Wove paper, no watermark. Top edges trimmed,
others untrimmed. Bound in brown cloth, front
and back covers and backbone embossed in gold
with names of contributors. A panel of brick red
on backbone reads up Christopher Morley:
Ex Libris

White jacket, front, back, and backstrip illustrating
books in color, the design of George Salter. Front
and back flaps describe the jacket and tell of the
artist.
  Printed by Haddon Craftsmen, Camden, N. J. in
edition of 5000. Another edition, entirely reset
and printed at the Fair, has an all-black title
page, the sketch in the Camden printing being
supplanted by a full-length double rule and the
two lines ("The most important autograph / in
a book, is Your Own"); while the ornamental
line beneath Morley's name was replaced by a
double rule. Also a change in the text of p. [53]
reduced the number of lines to fifteen from
seventeen in the first issue. Number of copies
printed at the Fair is unknown. The misprint
"Helen" for "Helm" on page [49] and on the
back cover appears in both printings and is not
a distinguishing feature of the first issue.

On May 4, 1938, Lippincott published an edition of
"Ex Libris" with a new title page, reading:

Ex Libris / [ornamental rule] / ["The most important autograph / in a book, is Your Own"] /
A Small Anthology / compiled by / Christopher
Morley / [ornamental rule] / J. B. Lippincott
Company / Philadelphia London Montreal
Text and binding are the same as those of the Fair
printing. The jacket is printed in black, notwith-
standing the statement on page [53], and the
original Salter drawing is retained with a change
in the wording. 1200 copies were printed.

FOOTNOTES FOR A CENTENNIAL
1936
Footnotes / For / A Centennial / By /
Christopher / Morley / [ornament, in red] / 1936 /
New York: Philip C. Duschnes
COLLATION: La. 8vo. Pp. [1-4]-5-14, consisting
of p. [1] title as above, in a single type rule box;
verso, top, Copyright 1936 by Christopher Morley;
bottom, Walpole Printing Office: Mount Vernon;
p. [3] Note / This poem was written for the / Centennial of Haverford Col- / lege, and first published in the / Saturday Review of Literature, /
October 14, 1933. In deference / to occasional
requests for sep- / arate copies, four hundred
are / now printed in this edition, / to be sold at
$1.50 each. Any / proceeds from the sale
thereof / are pledged to the Haverford / College
Endowment Fund. / Christopher Morley / June,
1936 / P.S. In order to make this / publication
unique, no copies / will be autographed.; verso
blank; pp. 5-14 half-title Footnotes For A / Centennial / (Haverford College, 1833-1933) / [orna-
ment, in red], followed by poem. Three blank
leaves at front, two at back.

Laid paper, watermarked Bay Path Book / Made
in U.S.A. Top edges trimmed, others untrimmed.
Bound in bright red cloth. Front has black panel,
stamped with gold rule borders, and lettering in

gold reading Footnotes For / A Centennial, in fancy and plain rule boxes.

Onion-skin jacket, no printing.
400 copies were published June 6, 1936. Some copies have the apostrophe after "Keats'" in the note at the bottom of page 14; others do not. The publisher states "obviously the apostrophe fell out while the work was being printed . . . . Which were bound first, which were distributed first, no man knows."

The poem appeared first in the "Saturday Review of Literature," October 14, 1933, and, a month later, in the "Haverford College Centenary," October 6th, 7th, 8th MCMXXXIII, pages 91-96 (Lee p. 231).

STREAMLINES
      1936
Christopher Morley / Streamlines / [publisher's device] / MCMXXVI / Doubleday, Doran & Co., Inc. / Garden City, New York
COLLATION: 8vo. Pp. [i-ii-(frontispiece not included in the pagination)-iii-viii]-ix-x-[xi-xiv] + 1-290, consisting of p. [i] fly title Streamlines; verso blank; frontispiece, half-tone, not included in pagination has recto blank; p. [iii] title as above; verso Printed at the Country Life Press, Garden City, N.Y., U.S.A. / Copyright, 1933, 1934, 1935, 1936 / By Christopher Morley / All Rights Reserved / First Edition; p. [v] dedication of six lines; verso blank; p. [vii] twelve lines of acknowledgments to publishers; verso blank; pp. ix-x Contents; p. [xi] list of illustrations; verso blank; p. [xiii] second fly title Streamlines; verso blank; pp. 1-290 text. Buff end papers.

Laid paper, no watermark. Top edges trimmed and stained magenta, other edges untrimmed.

Bound in light gray cloth. Front and back have
brick red rule design. Backbone has brick red
panel, reading, in gold letters, Christopher /
Morley / Stream- / Lines / Doubleday Doran

Jacket silver with shaded stripes front and backstrip, back and flaps white. Three zig zag panels
across the front read Christopher / Morley in
red panel, Streamlines in white relief, and seven-
line reader in gray panel. Two top panels on the
front cover carry over to the backstrip and read
Christopher / Morley and Stream- / Lines.
Bottom of backstrip reads Doubleday / Doran.
Back cover, publisher's advertisement, followed
by ornament in red. Front flap, reader for book;
back flap, publisher's advertisement.
Published November 1936, with a first printing
of 5300 copies. P. [vii] carries a bibliographical
note listing the first appearances of the essays
contained in the volume.

THOMAS BIRD MOSHER
1936
Thomas Bird Mosher / By Christopher Morley /
[printer's mark] / 1936 / The Attic House /
Christmastime
COLLATION: 18mo. Pp. [1-12], consisting of
p. [1] title as above; verso An essay from John
Mistletoe by Christopher / Morley, "borrowed"
by Emerson G. Wulling / and printed with pleasure
in the busy time of / the year for friends, because
the essay and the / man it speaks of are worth
special attention. / Waes Hael!; pp. [3-12] half-
title Thomas Bird Mosher / [rule], followed by
text.
Laid paper, no watermark. No covers. Stitched
with silk cord.

BARTLETT'S FAMILIAR QUOTATIONS
Eleventh Edition
1937

Familiar / Quotations / A Collection of Passages,
Phrases, / and Proverbs Traced to Their /
Sources in Ancient and / Modern Literature / By /
John Bartlett / Eleventh Edition / Revised and
Enlarged / Christopher Morley, Editor / Louella
D. Everett, Associate Editor / [publisher's de-
vice] / Boston / Little, Brown And Company /
1937

COLLATION: La. 8vo. Pp. [i-iv]-v-xv-[xvi-xviii]-
xix-xlviii + [1-2]-3-1578, consisting of p. [i] fly
title Familiar Quotations; verso blank; p. [iii] title
as above, box of six rules, the inner dotted; verso
nine lines of printing and copyright notice and
publisher's trade mark in fancy box containing six
lines; pp. v-[xvi] Preface To The Eleventh Edition,
signed Christopher Morley. / Roslyn Heights,
L.I. / May 22, 1937; p. [xvii] Facsimile Of Preface
To First Edition; verso blank; pp. xix-xx Preface
To the Ninth Edition, signed John Bartlett / Cambridge, 1891; pp. xxi-xxii Preface To The Tenth
Edition, signed Nathan Haskell Dole / Boston,
July, 1914; pp. xxiii-xlvii Index of Authors;
p. xlviii Anonymous And Collective Works And
Groups / Of Quotations; p. [1] second fly title
Familiar Quotations; verso blank; pp. 3-1128 text;
p. [1129] Index, followed by four line quotation
from Shakespeare; verso blank; pp. [1131]-1578
Index. One blank leaf at front, two at back.

Wove paper, unwatermarked. All edges trimmed.
Bound in red buckram with gold lettering and
decoration in dark blue embossed panel. Front
cover reads Familiar / Quotations / [ornament] /
John Bartlett, the whole enclosed in box of gold
rules. Backbone has seven ornamental bands in
gold, with dark blue embossed panels between the
second, third, and fourth bands, and reads Familiar / Quotations / John Bartlett / Edited by /
Christopher Morley / and / Louella D. Everett /
Little, Brown / and Company

Jacket of heavy yellow paper, overprinted in red-brown, with central panel in dark blue, enclosed in box, all lettering in yellow relief. Front reads Bartlett's / Familiar / Quotations / Eleventh Edition Edited by / Christopher Morley / and / Louella D. Everett / [ornament] / [six-line quotation from the Bible]. Backstrip same as backbone of book, except that lettering is in yellow relief. Back cover publisher's advertisement. Flaps describe the book.

Published December 3, 1937 with a first printing of 20,000 copies. A prospectus was issued several months before the book publication consisting of 18 pages of reading matter and 12 ruled blank pages. Copies vary as to content. Also issued was a 12 page pamphlet with reading matter different from that of the prospectus. The binding of the prospectus was similar to that of the book. The wrappers of the pamphlet were similar to the jacket of the book.

In 1944, Doubleday, Doran and Co., Inc. issued a reprint of the 11th ed. of Bartlett in its "DeLuxe ed" series.

BARTLETT'S FAMILIAR QUOTATIONS
Twelfth Edition
1948
Familiar Quotations / A Collection of Passages, Phrases and Proverbs, / Traced to Their Sources in Ancient and Modern / Literature by John Bartlett · Twelfth / Edition, Revised and Enlarged [ornaments] / [ornament] Christopher Morley · Editor / Louella D. Everett · Associate Editor / [publisher's device] / Little, Brown and Company · Boston · 1948
COLLATION: La. 8vo. Pp. [i-iv]-v-viii-[ix-x]-xi-xlii + [1-2]-3-1254-[1255-1256]-1257-1831-[1832], consisting of p. [i] fly title Familiar Quotations;

verso blank; p. [iii] title as above; verso seven
lines of copyright and rights notices, followed by
Published November 1948; fancy box, containing
six lines of publisher's announcement, followed by
line Printed In The United States Of America;
pp. v-viii Preface To The Twelfth Edition, signed
Christopher Morley / Roslyn Heights, N. Y. /
August 7, 1947; p. [ix] Preface, followed by 20
lines, in single-rule box, with line beneath Facsimile Of Preface To First Edition; verso blank;
pp. xi-xii Preface To The Ninth Edition, signed
John Bartlett / Cambridge, March, 1891; pp. xiii-
xlii Index Of Authors; p. [1] second fly title Familiar Quotations; verso blank; pp. 3-1254 text;
p. [1255] Index, followed by Shakespearean quotations; verso blank; pp. 1257-1831 Index; p. [1832]
blank. Three blank leaves at back.

Wove paper, unwatermarked. All edges trimmed,
top stained blue. Bound in red buckram, blue and
gold decorations. Front reads, in fancy box, Familiar / Quotations / [ornament] / John Bartlett.
Backbone, in gold ornamentation, reads in gold on
blue Familiar / Quotations / John Bartlett / Edited
by / Christopher Morley / and / Louella D.
Everett; at bottom, gold on red background, Little,
Brown / And Company

The jacket is of heavy white paper, overprinted in
red on front and backstrip. Front has central
panel in blue, enclosed in box composed of rules
and ornament in relief, and reads, in white relief,
[ornamental rule] / Bartlett's / Familiar / Quotations / [ornament] / Twelfth Edition Edited by /
Christopher Morley / and / Louella D. Everett /
[ornamental rule]. Backstrip same as backbone
except that lettering and ornament are in white
relief. Back cover, publisher's note about the new
edition. Front and back flaps describe the book.

Published November 8, 1948, with a first printing of 19,000 copies.

GOODBYE TO SPRING
1937

[Fancy type-set rule] / Goodbye / to Spring / [fancy type-set rule] / Christopher Morley / Philadelphia / J. B. Lippincott Company / 1937
COLLATION: 12mo. Pp. [1-6]-7-[16], consisting of p. [1] Briefcase Breviaries / 4; verso blank; p. [3] title as above; verso Copyright, 1937, by / Christopher Morley / First printed in / The Saturday Review of Literature / May 29, 1937 / Printed and Bound in the U.S.A. at the / American Book Bindery—Stratford Press, Inc.; p. [5] fly title [ornament] / Goodbye to Spring / [ornament]; verso The Knothole, May 20; pp. 7-15 text, all in italic; p. [16] blank. One blank leaf at front, one at back.

Wove paper, no watermark. All edges trimmed. Bound in fancy boards. Backbone has label reading down Goodbye to Spring
Onion-skin jacket.

Issued December 1937 with a first printing of 278 copies. Upon release from bindery it was discovered that the imprint read "New York" instead of "Philadelphia" as intended. With exception of 15 copies, the title page was removed and one reading "Philadelphia" was substituted by tipping in. Some changes were made in reprinting the "Saturday Review of Literature" article which appeared under the title "A Goodbye."

"IT'S A KIND OF A MEMORABILIA"
1937

"It's a Kind of a Memorabilia" / A Letter About / The Trojan Horse / written to / F. P. Frazier / (of J. B. Lippincott Company) / Confidential /

Not For Sale / Printed by Permission / October
1937
COLLATION: 12mo. Pp. [1-2]-3-16, consisting
of p. [1] title as above with lines 7 and 8 in double-
line brackets; verso Copyright 1937 by J. B.
Lippincott Company / Printed in U.S.A.; pp. 3-16
"It's a kind of a memorabilia"— Fuscus, followed
by text, and signed Christopher Morley.

Laid paper, unwatermarked. All edges trimmed.
Bound in French-fold terra-cotta heavy wrappers,
front reading "It's a kind of a Memorabilia" /
Christopher Morley.
   First printing of 2500 copies October 8, 1937.
1000 copies were bound as above; 1500 appeared
same as above but with white wrappers. The
letter also appeared as an advertisement in the
Saturday Review of Literature," November 27,
1937.

PREFACE TO "BARTLETT"
        1937
Preface / To / "Bartlett" / By / Christopher
Morley / [publisher's device] / Illustrated /
Boston / Little, Brown And Company / 1937
COLLATION: 12mo. Pp. [i-ii-(frontispiece leaf
not included in pagination)-vi] + [1-2]-[30], consisting of p. [i] fly title Preface / To "Bartlett";
verso blank; frontispiece leaf not included in
pagination with recto blank and verso half-tone of
John Bartlett; p. [iii] title as above; verso copyright 1937, By Little, Brown And Company, followed by three lines of copyright information,
First Edition / Published October 1937 / Printed
in the United States of America; p. [v] Illustrations; verso blank; p. [1] second fly title Preface /
To "Bartlett"; verso blank; pp. 3-28 text; p. 29
caption Publisher's Note, followed by 9 lines;
p. [30] blank. Eight illustrations including fron-

tispiece not included in pagination. One blank leaf
at back.

Laid paper. No watermark. All edges trimmed.
Bound in tan boards with parallel red and black
geometrical designs, cream panel on front cover
reading, in brown, Preface to "Bartlett" / by
Christopher Morley. Backbone of red cloth.
Issued in plain onion-skin dust jacket.
    This essay is a reprint of the preface to eleventh
edition of Bartlett's "Familiar Quotations" of
which Morley was Editor-in-Chief. Its initial
appearance was in the "Atlantic Monthly,"
August, 1937, under the title "Literature
Through A Knothole." This edition was published October 11, 1937, with a first printing of
1800 copies.

THE RAG-PICKER OF PARIS
        1937
The Rag-Picker Of / Paris / Or / The Modest
Modiste / By / Edward Stirling, Esq. / First
Produced At The Royal Surrey Theatre / London,
June 23, 1847 / Now Revised And Re-Edified By /
Christopher Morley / [publisher's device] / Phil-
adelphia / J. B. Lippincott Company / London
COLLATION: 12mo. Pp. [1-12]-120, consisting
of p. [1] fly title The Rag-Picker Of / Paris / Or /
The Modest Modiste / [ornament]; verso blank;
p. [3] title page as above; verso Copyright, 1937,
By / Christopher Morley / Made In The / United
States Of / America; p. [5] Program Note, followed
by twenty-five lines; verso blank; p. [7] The Rag-
Picker of Paris / [double rule] / Synopsis of
Scenes / (Paris: 1827-1847), followed by fifteen
lines; verso blank; p. [9] Characters / [double
rule], followed by twenty-six lines; verso blank;
p. [11] Prologue / [double rule]; verso blank;
pp. 13-120 text.

Wove paper, no watermark. Top edges trimmed, stained blue. Bottom edges trimmed; front edges untrimmed. Bound in light gray cloth. Backbone reads, in blue, The / Rag- / Picker / Of / Paris / Stirling / And / Morley / Lippincott.

The jacket is white overprinted on the front and backstrip in cream-gray. Front reads The / Rag-Picker / Of Paris / [mask of comedy] / A Play / Adapted By / Christopher Morley. Back advertizes other books by Morley. Backstrip reads same as backbone. Front flap reads as title page without imprint information and adds at bottom Jacket Design by Lydia Bacon / $1.00. Back flap has the Program Note used on p. [5].
    Published January 13, 1938 with a first printing of 1500 copies.

SIR KENELM READS IN BED
1937
Sir Kenelm Reads in Bed / [illustration black on green, showing cavaliers in front of bookstore] / by / Christopher Morley / Philip C. Duschnes · New York
COLLATION: 8vo. Eight unnumbered pages, consisting of p. [1] title as above; verso, Four hundred copies of this booklet / have been printed in December / nineteen thirty-seven for the friends / of Philip C. and Fanny Duschnes. / The illustration by Valenti Angelo. / The Marchbanks Press, New York; / Reprinted from the New York Evening Post, Dec. 18th, 1922 / Copyright 1937, by Christopher Morley; pp. [3-6] half-title Sir Kenelm Reads in Bed / By Christopher Morley, followed by text; p. [7] inset at corners, a buff card 7 3/4" x 4" with fancy red border reads To the Right Honourable / Edward Earl of Dorset / My Lord, followed by text, with subscript Your Lordships most humble / and obedient Servant, /

Kenelm Digby; verso blank. One blank leaf at front, one at back.

Wove paper, watermarked Canterbury [D in diamond figure] / Wove. All edges trimmed. Bound in heavy green wrappers. Front cover reads, in gold, Sir Kenelm Reads in Bed / By Christopher Morley, in box with gold ornamental borders. Silk stitched. No jacket.

THE TROJAN HORSE
         1937
The / Trojan / Horse / By Christopher / Morley / J. B. Lippincott Company / 1937
COLLATION: 12mo. Pp. [i-vi]-xii + 1-[250], consisting of p. [i] fly title The Trojan Horse; verso, a rust panel with the design of a Greek helmet in white relief beneath which is quoted Ever it was, and ever it shal bifalle, / That Love is he that alle thing may binde; / For may no man for-do the lawe of kind. / —Chaucer: Troilus and Criseyde, 1, 236, the whole surrounded by a border of fret in black; p. [iii] title as above in rust panel with border of fret; verso Copyright 1937, by Christopher Morley / First Edition / Printed in United States of America; p. [v] To / G. C. / Come Back And All Will Be Forgiven; verso blank; pp. vii-viii poem of eight stanzas entitled Recuyell / Of The / Histories of Troy; pp. ix-x The characters are:, followed by list of characters in the story; pp. xi-xii The chapters are:, followed by list of contents; pp. 1-248 text; p. [249] twenty seven lines dealing with the type design, composition, and cover design used in the book; verso blank. One blank leaf at back.

Laid paper, unwatermarked. All edges trimmed and top edges stained blue. Bound in rust cloth with backbone in blue. Front reads, in white

relief, The Trojan Horse, followed by a helmet
design in blue. Backbone reads in white relief
[double rule ornament] / The / Trojan / Horse /
By / Christopher / Morley / [double rule orna-
ment] / Lippincott.

The jacket is white. Front is overprinted in gold,
rust, and blue, with mixture of classic and modern
shown in the Trojan Horse, temple, modern sky-
scrapers, planes, costumes, etc. Front reads at
top The Trojan / Horse, and at bottom Christopher
Morley. Backstrip reads The / Trojan / Horse /
Christopher / Morley, and at bottom Lippincott.
Back has advertisement, printed in blue, of Morley
books published by Lippincott. Flaps have a note
about the novel.
There were 15,000 copies published November 24,
1937.

Sock and Buskin, Brown University dramatic
society, gave a world premier presentation of
"The Trojan Horse" on March 23-26, 1938.
Text was adapted from the novel by Brenton
Greene Meader (Brown, '39) and directed by
Professor Ben W. Brown of the Department
of English.

A dramatization of the novel produced at Roslyn,
L. I. is described in "Life," November 25, 1940.

Appeared in abbreviated serial form in the
"Saturday Review of Literature" August 7-
November 27, 1937.

ESOTERICA VINIANA
1938
Esoterica / Viniana / by / Christopher Morley /
[sketch in lavender of bottle and glass] / Privately
Printed / Lawrence Oakley Cheever / Christmas:
1938

COLLATION: 8vo. Twelve unnumbered pages, consisting of p. [1] blank; verso reproduction of page of manuscript headed Esoterica Viniana; p. [3] title as above; verso Reprinted with the permission of the author. / This piece originally appeared in the Satur- / day Review of Literature, issue of / June 9, 1934. Copyright 1934 by / Christopher Morley.; pp. [5-10] text, opening with three-line initial letter in lavender; p. [11] Colophon / This piece first came to my attention when I / purchased a packet of Morley autograph ma- / terial. It is reprinted here with his per- / mission / for Lawrence and Dorothy Cheever. It has / been hand-set in Centaur and Arrighi types / by Carroll D. Coleman at The Prairie Press, / Muscatine, Iowa. An edition of one hundred copies has been printed and the type distributed. / Title page illustration and initial letter / drawn by A. M. Johnson; p. [12] blank. The type of each page is enclosed in a rule box, printed in red.

Wove paper, watermarked Worthy Brochure. Top and bottom edges trimmed, front edges untrimmed. Bound in fancy red-brown wrappers, front reading, in rule-and-ornament box, Esoterica / Viniana / [ornament] / Christopher Morley. Stitched with red-brown silk cord.
   Page [6] lines 1 and 2 read incorrectly "knowing some" instead of "some knowing."

FRIENDS OF THE LIBRARY
1938
Friends of / The Library / A Soliloquy uttered by / Christopher Morley / at a meeting of the Friends of the Library, Dr. John H. Finley / being chairman, New York City, June 23, 1937 / [rule] / [printer's device] / [rule] / Reprinted with the permission of the Author and of the / Saturday Review of Literature by / The Marchbanks Press /

New York, the whole in a rule box with a double
rule at the top.
COLLATION: 16mo. Pp. [1-2]-3-10-[11-12], consisting of p. [1] title as above; verso blank; pp. 3-
10 half-title Friends of the Library, followed by
text; p. [11] blank; verso Designed by Edward
Alonzo Miller, and printed by / The Marchbanks
Press, New York

Wove paper, no watermark. All edges trimmed.
Bound in light blue wrappers, front reading same
as title page.
Issued August 17, 1938, in a first printing of
3000 copies. Reprinted from "Saturday Review
of Literature," July 3, 1937. The address
appears in abridged form in the American Library Association "Bulletin," October 15, 1937.

HISTORY OF AN AUTUMN
1938
Christopher Morley / History / Of / An Autumn /
[ornament] / Philadelphia and New York / J. B.
Lippincott Company / 1938
COLLATION: 16mo. Pp. [i-ii-(frontispiece leaf
not included in the pagination)-vi]-vii-ix-[x-xii] +
1-[82], consisting of p. [i] fly title History / Of /
An Autumn; verso blank; frontispiece with caption
Downing Street, September, 1938, not included in
the pagination; p. [iii] title as above; verso CL /
Copyright, 1938, By / Christopher Morley / A
brief portion of this history was first printed / in
the Saturday Review of Literature, October 15,
1938 / Printed in U.S.A.; p. [v] "Rededicate" /
L.J.M.; verso blank; p. vii-ix half-title History /
Of / An Autumn / (1938) / [rule], followed by a
series of quotations; p. [x] blank; p. [xi] second
fly title History / Of / An Autumn; verso blank;
pp. 1-81 text; p. [82] blank. One blank leaf at back.

Laid paper, unwatermarked. Top and bottom edges trimmed, front edges untrimmed, and top edges stained rust. Bound in rust colored cloth, front reading, in gold, History / Of / An Autumn. The lettering on front cover is enclosed in a box with gold borders, the lower border of which is ornamental. Backbone reads down, in gold, Christopher   History of An Autumn Morley   Lippincott

The jacket is buff. Within box of multiple red rules, front reads Christopher / Morley / History / Of An / Autumn / followed by author's six line note about the book. Backstrip reads within box of multiple red rules same as backbone. Back has an advertisement of "The Trojan Horse" in red and black. Back flap advertises "Morley's Magnum," and front flap has a note about the book. Issued November 30, 1938, with a first printing of 5000 copies. The words "Printed in U.S.A." on the verso of the title page were, by mistake, omitted in the first printing. A linotype slug was used in lieu of a rubber stamp and the bound books were stamped. The inking is different from the rest of the copyright page and is sometimes off center. Some copies escaped the imprinting with the linotype slug. In the second printing (December, 1938), the linotype slug was inserted in the form and the inking matches the rest of the copyright page.

MORLEY'S MAGNUM
          1938
Morley's Magnum / [rule] / Swiss Family Manhattan / Rehearsal / Mandarin In Manhattan / The Romany Stain / Chimneysmoke / Hasta La Vista / [rule] / By Christopher Morley / [rule] / [publisher's device] / [rule] / Philadelphia New York / J. B. Lippincott Company / London Toronto / [rule]

COLLATION: 8vo. Pp. [i-viii] + 1-208,* consisting of p. [i] fly title Morley's / Magnum / [ornament]; verso blank; p. [iii] title as above; verso Copyright, 1917, 1919, 1920, 1921, 1922, 1924, 1926, 1927, 1928, / 1930, 1931, 1932, 1933, 1934, 1935, By Christopher Morley / Made In The United States Of America; p. [v] Contents, followed by six lines; verso blank; p. [vii] second fly title Swiss Family Manhattan; verso Swiss Family Manhattan, followed by Morley's note on how, when, and where this book was written [thirty-two lines]; pp. 1-208 text of first story.
 [*From this point on, the pagination is irregular, due to the use of plates of earlier books. See front flap of jacket]
Wove paper, unwatermarked. All edges trimmed, top stained green. Bound in red cloth, front reading Morley's Magnum / Christopher Morley. Backbone reads Morley's / Magnum / Christopher / Morley / Lippincott

White jacket with green on front and backstrip. Front design shows six sketches of miniature books shot from a champagne bottle, with the title of each printed in the figure. In addition, the front cover reads Morley's / Magnum, with a six-line description in right bottom corner. Back advertizes other books by Morley. Backstrip reads Christopher / Morley's / Magnum / [ornament] / Lippincott. Front flap has a note about the "Magnum"; back flap advertizes "The Trojan Horse."
 This reprint is the second Omnibus collection of Morley's writings, the first being "Fifth Avenue Bus" published in 1933. The first printing appeared May 12, 1938 and consisted of 5070 copies. For the "Omnibus" Morley wrote a new preface to each work included telling how and why and where and when each book was written. This information is printed on green paper and

inserted before each work, title on recto and
the introductory Morley article on verso.

"NO CRABB NO CHRISTMAS"
1938
"No Crabb / No Christmas" / By / Christopher
Morley / [holly wreath in green and red] / The
Black Cat Press · 1938 / Chicago, Illinois
COLLATION: 18mo. Pp. [1-6] + 7-20-[21-22],
consisting of p. [1] fly leaf; verso blank; p. [3] fly
title "No Crabb—No Christmas"; verso blank;
p. [5] title as above, surrounded by a type ornament border; verso Copyrighted 1938, By Christopher Morley / First Edition / Reprinted From
Saturday Review of Literature; pp. 7-20 text,
opening with headpiece of five Christmas bells
printed in red; p. [21] blank; verso Colophon / Of
this first edition 225 copies have / been printed
of which only 25 copies / are for sale. Set in
Linotype Caslon / by the Falcon Press and printed
on / hand-made Berestoke paper by Louis / Graf.
Completed at Chicago, Illinois, / during the month
of December, 1938, / Design & Typography by /
Norman W. Forgue. One blank leaf at front and
one at back.

Hand-made wove paper, watermarked Free Folk.
All edges untrimmed. Bound in green cloth, white
label on front reading "No Crabb / No
Christmas" / Christopher Morley, in box of type
ornaments. Pages uncut.
No jacket.

ON THE RETURN OF A BOOK LENT TO A
FRIEND
1938
On the Return of / A Book / Lent to a Friend /
[ornament] / Black Cat Press / 1938
COLLATION: 32mo. Eight unnumbered pages,
consisting of p. [1] title as above, enclosed in rule

box, the ornament and inner rule in red; pp. [2-3]
blank; pp. [4-5] text, caption, in red, On the Return of a / Book Lent to a Friend; pp. [6-7] blank;
p. [8] 50 copies / of this miniature keepsake /
have been printed / from / Linotype Caslon / on /
Worthy Hand & Arrows / by / The Black Cat
Press / at Chicago / 1938. One blank leaf at
front, one at back.

Laid paper, watermarked Worthy Hand & Arrows.
Bound in heavy blue wrappers, front cover read-
ing up On the Return of a Book Lent to a Friend.
Stitched with silk cord.
    Issued July 1938 and sent to personal friends
of the Black Cat Press and of Norman W.
Forgue, Director. The sketch appeared also in
"The Haunted Bookshop," (1919) p. 57, and in
"The Book Detektive," (q.v.).

A SHERLOCK HOLMES CROSS-WORD PUZZLE
            1938
A / Sherlock Holmes / Cross-Word Puzzle / By /
Mycroft Holmes / Recently Brought to Light / By
Tobias Gregson, / Late of Scotland Yard / And
Transmitted by Him to / Christopher Morley /
[fancy rule] / Privately Printed / 1938
COLLATION: 12mo. Pp. [1-2]-3-5-[6-8], consisting of p. [1] title as above, enclosed in fancy type
ornament border; verso Reprinted from the Saturday / Review of Literature of May / 19, 1934,
with the permission / of Christopher Morley;
pp. 3-5 fancy headpiece, two-line caption A Sherlock Holmes / Cross-word Puzzle, text opening
with two-line initial; p. [6] Cross-Word 221 B /
(Baker Street Irregulars), followed by puzzle
diagram, signed Mycroft Holmes; p. [7] questions
to puzzle, printed in two columns; p. [8] headpiece,
fancy capital S / Thirty-nine copies of A / Sherlock Holmes Cross- / word Puzzle have been /
printed for the Friends / of Walter Klinefelter, /

Christmas, 1938, by the / Southworth-Anthoensen /
Press, Portland, Maine. / This is Copy Number /
Tailpiece, fancy capital H.

Wove paper, unwatermarked. Top and bottom
edges trimmed, front edges untrimmed. Bound in
heavy plum-colored wrappers, front cover reading
A Sherlock Holmes / Cross-Word Puzzle, in box
of type ornaments.
   This work was written by Frank V. Morley,
Christopher contributing the introductory paragraph. It first appeared under the title "Sherlock Holmes Crossword" in the "Saturday Review of Literature" May 19, 1934. Also published under the title "Sherlock Holmes Cross-
word" in Vincent Starrett's "221B Studies in
Sherlock Holmes" (q.v.) and correctly attributed
to F. V. Morley.

FOUR FAVORITE BOOKS
        1939
[double rule] / Four Favorite Books By / Christopher Morley / Four Volumes In One / Parnassus on Wheels / The Haunted Bookshop / Where
the Blue Begins / Thunder on the Left / [rule] /
[sketch of Morley head] / [rule] / Garden City
Publishing Co., Inc. / New York / [double rule]
COLLATION: 8vo. Pp. [i-vi] + [1-2]-3-190,* consisting of p. [i] fly title Four Favorite Books By /
Christopher Morley; verso blank; p. [iii] title as
above; verso [printer's device] / CL / 1939 /
Garden City Publishing Co., Inc. / Copyright 1917,
1918, 1919, 1922, 1923, 1925, 1934 / By Christopher Morley / All Rights Reserved / Printed In
The / United States Of America; p. [v] fly title
Parnassus On Wheels; verso To / H. B. F. and
H. F. M. / "Trusty, dusky, vivid, true"; pp. [1]-
190 text of "Parnassus on Wheels." The last
page of the volume p. [274] contains in a box a list
of Other Books / By The Same Author

[*From this point on, the pagination is irregular, due to the employment of plates used in earlier books]
Wove paper, unwatermarked. All edges trimmed, top stained red. Bound in red buckram, front carries blind stamp in outline of Morley head. Backbone reads, in gold, in black panel Four / Favorite / Books By / Christopher / Morley

11,500 copies of the first printing appeared July 1939. The second story reprinted in the volume, "The Haunted Bookshop," is preceded by a note from the publisher. "Four Favorite Books" was reprinted by Garden City in 1941 in the "de luxe eds." series.

GOUDIAMUS IGITUR
1939
To Frederic W. Goudy / On His Seventy-fourth Birthday / Goudiamus [open-face type] / Igitur [open-face type] / [ornament] / By / Christopher / Morley / March Eighth ~ MCM · XXX · IX
COLLATION: 16mo. Sixteen unnumbered pages, consisting of p. [1] title as above, all type except the first two lines and last line printed in red, backed by horizontal lines in blue; pp. [2-4] blank; p. [5] Goudiamus Igitur, in red / He who should plant honeysuckle round Trajan's column, / would not be thought to adorn, but to disgrace it.—Mrs. Thrale / Anecdotes of Dr. Johnson / [ornament, in red] / first two stanzas of the poem, four lines each; pp. [6-7] blank; pp. [8-9] eight stanzas of the poem; pp. [10-11] blank; p. [12] final two stanzas of the poem; pp. [13-15] blank; p. [16] printer's device of the Overbrook Press, in black and red, formerly used by Margaret B. Evans / & Elizabeth Mann / March eighth: Mcmxxxix / The printers express gratitude to Frank Altschul, Esquire, / for turning over to them the resources of the Overbrook Press. Two blank leaves at front, two at back.

Laid paper, watermarked C M Fabriano—Italy.
Issued uncut. Bound in heavy gray blue wrappers,
front bearing white label reading [line of orna-
ments] / Goudiamus Igitur / By Christopher
Morley / Privately Printed: Mcm · xxx · ix /
[line of ornaments]
   There were 24 copies of the signature given the
above binding, issued March 8, 1939.

KITTY FOYLE
               1939
Christopher Morley / [rule] / Kitty / Foyle /
[rule] / J. B. Lippincott Company / Philadelphia
New York Toronto
COLLATION: 8vo. Pp. [1-8]-9-[340], consisting
of p. [1] fly title Kitty Foyle; verso blank; p. [3]
title as above, the words Kitty Foyle appearing in
large red script; verso Copyright, 1939, By /
Christopher Morley / First Edition / Printed In
The United States Of America; p. [5] four-line
quotation in italic from—George Saintsbury, The
English Novel (1892).; verso blank; p. [7] second
fly title Kitty Foyle; verso blank; pp. 9-[340] text.
Buff end papers.

Laid paper, no watermark. Top and bottom edges
trimmed, front edges untrimmed. Top edges
stained red. Bound in green cloth. Front reads,
in white and in script capitals K F. Backbone
reads, in white, Christopher / Morley / Kitty /
Foyle / Lippincott

Jacket is white overprinted in black and green on
front and backstrip. Front reads, in black and
white, Kitty / Foyle, and in a black panel at the
bottom, in gold, A Novel By / Christopher Morley.
Back carries advertisement of author's books in
black and green. Backstrip has black panel at
top, reading, in gold, Morley / Kitty / Foyle /
Lippincott. Front and back flaps carry reader of

the book, the back flap closing with the words This
novel has not been serialized / and none of it has
been printed before / in any form
  The first printing, October 26, 1939, consisted
of 16,250 copies. On June 21, the publisher
issued 900 pamphlets, of 16 pages, in wrappers,
carrying the first chapter of the forthcoming
book. The pamphlet carries a different title
page from the book when later published. On
the same date there were 200 full, dummy copies
issued, containing the first chapter complete.

"Kitty Foyle" was issued after publication in
serial form in the Philadelphia "Evening Bulletin," December 9-30, 1940; also it was reprinted in the following series: "Novels of Dis-
tinction" series, Grosset and Dunlap, 1940;
"Madison Sq. B'ks." series, Grosset, 1943;
Penguin Books, 1944; and "Tower Bks." series,
World Publishing Company, 1944.

The screen rights were purchased by RKO and
the movie "Kitty Foyle," first released December 27, 1940, won an Academy Award. A
condensed version of the movie script appears
in "Movie Mirror" v. 18:26-27, 70, 72, 74, December, 1940, continued in "Photoplay" 18:42-
43, 83-86, January, 1941.

The first stage dramatization was made August
13-15, 1942, at the Michiana Shores Theatre in
Chicago under the direction of Letitia V.
Barnum. The play version appeared in print in
1942 as follows:
  Christopher Morley's / Kitty Foyle / A
  Comedy in Three Acts, Dramatized / from the
  Novel, / by / Christopher Sergel / [orna-

ment] / The Dramatic Publishing Company /
Chicago
12mo. 144 pages. Wove paper. Heavy buff
wrappers.

LETTERS OF ASKANCE
          1939
Christopher Morley / Letters Of / Askance /
[publisher's device] / Philadelphia New York /
J. B. Lippincott Company / London Toronto
COLLATION: 8vo. Pp. [1-6]-7-9-[10-(a leaf not
included in the pagination)] + 11-[318], consisting
of p. [1] fly title Letters of Askance; verso blank;
p. [3] title as above; verso Copyright, 1939, By /
Christopher Morley / Made In The / United States
Of / America; p. [5] For Blythe / From Whom I
Borrowed / The Title; verso blank; pp. 7-9 Contents; p. [10] blank; second fly title Letters of
Askance, and verso blank not included in the
pagination; pp. 11-[315] text; pp. 316-[318] Mani-
fest, telling where the essays contained in the
book were originally printed and contains notes on
two of the essays. One blank leaf at the back.
Buff end papers.

Laid paper, no watermark. Top and bottom edges
trimmed and top stained green. Front edges untrimmed. Bound in green cloth, blind stamping
forms a border on the front cover. Backbone
reads, in gold, Christopher / Morley / Letters /
Of / Askance / Lippincott

Jacket is heavy cream paper, front carries a picture of ink bottle and quill pen in black and green
and reads Letters Of / Askance / Christopher /
Morley. Back advertises other books by Morley
published by Lippincott. Backstrip has ink bottle
and quill pen similar to front and reads Letters /
Of / Askance / Morley / Lippincott. Front flap
carries a note on "Letters of Askance"; back flap

reviews "History Of An Autumn."
First printing consisted of 3,500 copies published May 4, 1939.

PASSIVITY PROGRAM
1939
Christopher Morley / Passivity / Program /
1939 / [rule] / The Argus Book Shop, Inc. /
Chicago
COLLATION: La. 8vo. Pp. [1-4]-5-10-[11-12]-
27-[28], consisting of p. [1] fly title Passivity
Program; verso blank; p. [3] title as above, with
lines 2, 3, and 5 in red; verso Copyright 1939 By
The Saturday Review Of Literature / Copyright
1939 By The Argus Book Shop, Inc. / Publisher's
Note / [seven lines] / Printed In The U.S.A.; pp. 5-
10 Introduction, printed in red between double
rules of type ornaments, followed by text and
signed Ben Abramson; p. [11] second fly title
Passivity Program; verso blank; pp. 13-27 half-
title Passivity Program printed in red between
double rules of type ornaments followed by text
which opens with initial in red; p. [28] blank. One
blank leaf at front, one at back.

Wove paper, no watermark. All edges trimmed.
Bound in decorated boards, black and white wire
mesh design, with five heavy black and red bands
running from front to back cover at the center.
Front has a pasted label in the shape of a suit-
case, black with white trim, which reads in white
relief Passivity / Program / · / Christopher
Morley
No jacket.
Condensation of a lecture given April 1939 at
Adelphi College, Garden City, Long Island,
"Passivity Program" had its first printing in
the "Saturday Review of Literature," April 29,
1939. It appeared in form above, with additions

47

and changes, October 25, in an edition of 2000 copies.

TO FRA GIOVANNI AT PONTASSIEVE, NEAR FIRENZE
1939
[Medallion portrait in colors, in scroll border] / To Fra Giovanni at Pontassieve, near Firenze. COLLATION: La. 8vo. Four-page leaflet, unnumbered, consisting of p. [1] the title as above followed by the lines Under secure cover, these:, followed by text with the initial letters at head of each paragraph printed in brown; p. [2] blank; p. [3] text continued from p. [1], signed Your Allagia. / Christmas Day, MDCIII.; p. [4] Written by Christopher Morley as a suitable reply to a / Christmas letter from Fra Giovanni to the Contessina / Allagia which was composed by Ernest Temple Hargrove. / Copyright Mdccccxxxix by Christopher Morley / Printed by the Yale University Press

Heavy wove paper, no watermark. Top and bottom edges trimmed. No covers.
The letter was first printed, 1150 copies, November, 1939.

FRIENDS, ROMANS . . . .
1940
Friends, Romans . . . . / [rule] / by / Christopher Morley / [device of The Ampersand Club] / [rule] / The Ampersand Club / Minneapolis And St. Paul / & 1940 &
COLLATION: 12mo. Pp. [i-vi]-vii-xii-[xiii-xiv] + 1-[22], consisting of p. [i] fly title Friends, Romans . . . .; verso blank; p. [iii] title as above, the device of The Ampersand Club in rust; verso Copyright, 1940, By Christopher Morley; p. [v] quotation from Morley in italics topped by a rule and followed by a credit line Saturday Review

Of Literature / December 23, 1939; verso blank;
pp. vii-ix opening with a row of fancy type ornaments and rule beneath in rust followed by the
words Dear Chris and ending Sincerely, / Paul C.
Hillestad, / Secretary, The Ampersand Club;
verso blank; pp. xi-xii introduction opening on
p. xi with a headpiece of fancy type ornaments
and rule beneath in rust, the letters MPL in the
center of the headpiece, and ending p. xii Carl
Vitz / Librarian, Minneapolis Public Library /
& / Member, The Ampersand Club; p. [xiii] second
fly title Friends, Romans . . . .; verso eighteen
lines, remarks of Dr. Guy Stanton Ford; pp.
&1&-&21& text opening with a row of fancy type
ornaments between rules in rust and with the
letters CM in the center; p. [22] Friends, Romans . . . Has Been Printed / From Granjon Type
Upon Worthy / Permanent Book With Endpapers, /
Labels, & Jacket Of Linweave Text. / Five Hundred & Thirty-Five Copies / Have Been Issued By
The Ampersand / Club Of Minneapolis And St.
Paul. One blank leaf at front, one at back. Blue
endpapers.

Wove paper, no watermark. All edges trimmed.
Bound in royal blue cloth. Front has pale blue
label and reads, in brown, between heavy brown
rules Friends, Romans . . . . / Christopher
Morley. Backbone has pale blue label and reads
down [rule, in brown] Friends, Romans . . . .
[rule, in brown] Morley [rule, in brown].

The jacket is pale blue. Front reads, in brown,
Friends, Romans . . ., followed by, in blue, By
Christopher Morley, followed by a list of the
author's other writings. Back carries, in blue,
a note about the book and the device of The Ampersand Club, in brown. Backstrip reads down, in
blue, Friends Romans . . . & Christopher Morley
& The Ampersand Club. Front flap describes

the occasion of Morley's talk. Back flap is blank.
535 copies were printed September 30, 1940.
Included with copies for members of the Ampersand Club was a facsimile letter from Morley to Paul Hillestad, Secretary of the Club,
dated May 1, 1940, begging off autographing
copies for the Ampersands. A card 3 3/8" x
5 1/2" was sent out by the Club announcing the
publication of "Friends, Romans . . . ."

HUMAN BEING
            1940
[Publisher's device] / Human / Being / A Story
by / Christopher / Morley / With a new Introduction by / The Author / Modern Library · New
York, the whole except publisher's device and the
last line in a rule box.
COLLATION: 12mo. Pp. [i-viii]-[six unnumbered
pages]-ix-xii-[xiii-xiv] + [1]-[356], consisting of
p. [i] fly title Human Being, with two lines followed
by a rule above, and a rule followed by six lines
below; verso blank; p. [iii] title as above; verso
Copyright, 1932, By Christopher Morley / Copyright 1940, By Random House, Inc. / First Modern
Library Edition, 1940 / [publisher's device] / six
lines enclosed in rule box; p. [v] Affectionately
Dedicated To, followed by nine lines; verso blank;
p. [vii] six introductory lines; verso blank; unnumbered page headed A Note On The Author Of /
Human Being; verso blank; four unnumbered pages
headed Introduction, signed at the end Christopher
Morley / April 8, 1940; pp. ix-xii [double rule] /
Contents; p. [xiii] second fly title Human Being;
verso blank; pp. [1]-350 text; pp. [351-55] contain
a complete list of titles in The Modern Library;
p. [356] blank. Fancy gray end papers.

Wove paper, no watermark. All edges trimmed,
top edges stained blue-gray. Bound in red cloth.
Front has black panel edged in gold and reads, in

50

gold, Human Being / [ornament] / Morley, the
whole surrounded by a rule box in gold and containing publisher's device in bottom right corner.
Backbone has black panel edged in gold and topped
by publisher's device. The panel reads down, in
gold, Human Being by Christopher Morley (two
lines), beneath which is [ornament, in gold] /
Modern / Library

Jacket is white overprinted in black and orange
on front and backstrip. Front reads, in white
relief Christopher Morley / Human / Being / A
Novel / A Modern Library Book. The title above
is edged in gold. Above last line is a white panel
with inner three-quarter box rule, in gold, containing author's note of six lines and signed—Christopher Morley. Back advertises Modern Library
Books in fancy design in gold, white relief, and
black. Backstrip reads at top Christopher / Morley, and at bottom 74 / Modern / Library. The
center of backstrip reads down, in white relief,
Human Being, the whole surrounded by box rule
topped by the publisher's device in gold. Front
flap has a note on the book and on The Modern
Library series extending on the back flap. Inside
of jacket advertises Modern Library books.
    This edition has a publisher's note about Mor-
ley and a new introduction by him which did not
appear in the original edition. The first printing
consisting of 5000 copies appeared October 10,
1940. First line on page 287 contains "wanted"
for "want." Same typographical error is to be
found in the first edition of "Human Being"
(1932), and in the special binding edition (Lee,
#108), but was corrected in the English edition
published by Faber & Faber, Ltd., 1933.

TROJAN HORSE
1941
The Trojan Horse / A / Contemporary / Drama /

Laid In / 1185 B. C. / By Christopher Morley /
[publisher's device] / Random House · New York
COLLATION: 12mo. Pp. [i-ii-(inserted frontispiece)-iv]-v-xviii + [1-2]-3-[200], consisting of
p. [i] fly title The Trojan Horse; verso blank; inserted frontispiece showing on verso cast of
Roslyn, L. I. production; p. [iii] title as above;
verso First Printing / [eleven lines of copyright
information] / Copyright, 1937, 1941, By Christopher Morley / Photographs Courtesy of Karger-
Pix / Manufactured in the United States of America; p. v The Characters; p. vi The Action (acts,
scenes, and captions); pp. vii-viii describes
briefly the Roslyn, L. I. production and lists the
actors: pp. ix-xiv Foreword, signed Christopher
Morley / Roslyn, Long Island, / June, 1941;
pp. xv-xviii Director's Note On Musical / Background, signed David Lowe; p. [1] Act One; verso
blank; pp. 3-199 text, with pages between acts
unnumbered but included in the pagination; p. [200]
blank. The three inserted illustrations, not included in the pagination are in half-tone, on calendared paper. One blank leaf at front, two at
back.

Laid paper. Publisher's device used as watermark. All edges trimmed and top edge stained
blue. Bound in royal blue. Backbone reads, in
gold, [eight rules] / The / Trojan / Horse / · /
Christopher / Morley / · / · / · / [publisher's de-
vice] / Random / House / [nine rules]

Jacket of heavy cream paper. Front has border
and panel in aquamarine, the panel surrounded by
black rule box broken at right bottom corner by
publisher's device. Panel reads, in relief, The /
Trojan / Horse / A Play By / Christopher / Morley / A Random House Play. Back carries advertisement of Random House books in black and aquamarine. Backstrip reads [rule] / [rule] / The /

Trojan / Horse / [ornament] / Christopher / Morley / [publisher's device] / Random / House / [rule] / [rule]. Front flap carries a note about the play by the author. Back flap advertises "The Modern Library."
The first printing, consisting of 2000 copies, appeared September 17, 1941.

THE GUTENBERG ADDRESS
1942
The Gutenberg / Address / [two-colored cut of eagle and open book]
COLLATION: 8vo. Eight unnumbered pages, consisting of p. [1] title as above on the front cover with cut of eagle and open book in brown and blue against white; verso Christopher Morley Wrote / The Gutenberg Address / That The Proceeds From / Its Sale Could Be Used / To Furnish Books For The / American Armed Forces. / Capt. Barse Miller Made / The Cover Drawing And Bryan-Brandenburg Co. / Furnished Engravings. / Printed In Los Angeles / By Anderson & Ritchie: / The Ward Ritchie Press / July 1942 / [rule] / Copyright 1942 by Christopher Morley; pp. [3-7] text, with the closing words of the text printed in capitals in a rule box on page [7], signed outside the rule box Christopher Morley; p. [8] blank.

Heavy wove paper, not watermarked. All edges trimmed. The front cover is the title page.
2000 copies of this brochure were printed in July, 1942.

THOROFARE
1942
Thorofare / Christopher Morley / New York / Harcourt, Brace And Company
COLLATION: 8vo. Pp. [i-x] + [1-2]-3-[470], consisting of p. [i] fly title Thorofare; verso blank;

p. [iii] title as above; verso Copyright, 1942, By /
Harcourt, Brace And Company, Inc. / [three
lines] / first edition / Printed in the United States
of America; p. [v] The past is always present:
yet it is not what was, / but whatever seems to
have been. / —G. K. Chesterton / You do yet
taste / some subtleties o' the isle / —Prospero;
verso blank; p. [vii] For / Uncles And Aunts;
verso blank; p. [ix] Contents; verso blank; p. [1]
second fly title Thorofare; verso blank; pp. 3-469
text; p. [470] blank.

Wove paper, unwatermarked. Top edges trimmed
and stained green. Bottom edges trimmed, front
edges untrimmed. Bound in royal blue cloth.
Backbone reads, in yellow, Christopher / Morley /
Thoro- / fare / Harcourt, Brace / and Company

The jacket is white, overprinted on front and back-
strip in royal blue with multi-colored design on the
front. Front reads, in white relief, Thorofare, in
yellow relief, A Novel By / Christopher / Morley.
Back carries nineteen lines with Morley auto-
graphic facsimile, a story to promote the sale of
War Bonds. Backstrip reads, in white relief,
Thorofare / Christopher / Morley / Harcourt,
Brace / and Company. Front and back flaps, in
blue, carry a description of the book.
The first printing of 20,000 copies appeared
November 19, 1942.

THE MIDDLE KINGDOM
1944
The Middle Kingdom / Poems, 1929-1944 / By
Christopher Morley / [rule] / Er Minnet Iemer
Deste Baz / Swer Von Minnen Etewaz / Hoeret
Singen Oder Lesen / —Walter Von Der Vogel-
weide / [rule] / Harcourt, Brace And Company /
1944
COLLATION: 8vo. Pp. [i-viii]-ix-x + [1-2]-3-118,

consisting of p. [i] fly title The Middle Kingdom; verso Also by the Same Author, followed by nine book titles; p. [iii] title as above; verso Copyright, 1944, By / Harcourt, Brace And Company, Inc. / [three lines] / first edition / [sketch of eagle] / A Wartime Book, followed by five lines of printing notices; p. [v] In Thought Of / Don Marquis / 1878-1937; verso blank; p. [vii] Note, followed by sixteen lines signed C. M. / Roslyn Heights, L. I. / May 5, 1944; verso blank; pp. ix-x Contents; p. [1] second fly title The Middle Kingdom; verso blank; pp. 3-118 text.

Wove paper, no watermark. All edges trimmed. Bound in dark blue cloth. Front cover reads, in red, The Middle / Kingdom. Backbone reads down, in red, Christopher Morley The Middle Kingdom Harcourt, Brace / And Company

The jacket is gray, overprinted in red on the front. Front cover reads Christopher Morley / The Middle / Kingdom / Poems 1929-1944, the title in white relief and the remainder in blue. Back cover carries a review of "The Middle Kingdom" by William Rose Benét. Backstrip reads same as backbone, the title in red and the remainder in blue. Front flap carries a note about the book; back flap carries excerpts from reviews of "Thorofare."
  First published October 5, 1944, in an edition of 3,500 copies.

MORLEY'S VARIETY
    1944
Morley's Variety / [Forum Books device] / A Selection From the Writings Of / Christopher Morley, Made By / Louis Greenfield, And Published / In Cleveland And New York By / The World Publishing Company
COLLATION: 8vo. Pp. [i-iv] + [1-6]-7-636, con-

sisting of p. [i] fly title Morley's Variety; verso
blank; p. [iii] title as above; verso twenty lines of
printing, composition, and copyright notices and
the line First Printing October 1944; p. [1] Acknowledgments, followed by six lines; verso blank;
pp. [3-6] Contents; pp. 7-13 A Lowbrow Introduction, signed Louis Greenfield / May 1944; p. [14]
blank; pp. 15-17 A Letter to the Editor / from /
Christopher Morley, signed Christopher Morley;
p. [18] blank; p. [19] second fly title Complete
Novels; p. [20] blank; pp. 21-636 text.

Light weight wove paper, no watermark. Top and
bottom edges trimmed and top edges stained
green, front edges untrimmed. Bound in green
buckram. Front reads, in green, in a lighter shade
green panel with broken edges Morley's Variety.
Backbone reads Edited By / Louis Greenfield /
Morley's / Variety / [Forum Books device] The
World / Publishing Company, the title enclosed in
a light green panel.

The jacket, designed by Leo Manso, is white overprinted in green with ornamental pink design on
the front and backstrip. Front reads Morley's
Variety / [rule] / A selection / from the writings
of / Christopher / Morley / made by Louis Greenfield / containing / Three complete novels /
Thunder On The Left · Trojan Horse · Kathleen /
Selections from novels / Thorofare · Kitty Foyle ·
Human Being / Short stories, such as / The Red
And White Girdle · The Arrow / Also essays,
poems, and plays. Back has photograph of Morley and a quotation from the editor's introduction
which continues on the back flap. Backstrip reads
Morley's / Variety / A selection / from the writings of / Christopher / Morley / made by Louis
Greenfield / [Forum Books device] / F-63. Front
flap has a notice about the book, with the last line
reading Jacket Design By Leo Manso.

The first printing consisted of 10,000 copies.
"Soft Shoulders," a play, described in the
editor's introduction (p. 12) as having its first
printing in this book, does not appear in the text.

MORLEY'S VARIETY
1944
SPECIAL LIMITED EDITION
Morley's Variety / [profile sketch of the author] /
A Selection From The Writings Of / Christopher
Morley, Made By / Louis Greenfield, And Pub-
lished / In Cleveland And New York By / The
World Publishing Company
COLLATION: La. 8vo. Pp. [i-iv] + [1-6]-7-636,
consisting of p. [i] fly title Morley's Variety /
This Special Edition Of Morley's Variety Is
Limited / To 875 Numbered Copies For Private
Distribution / To Friends Of The Publisher. /
Printing And Binding By The Haddon Craftsmen /
Typography And Design By Abe Lerner. No.   ;
verso blank; p. [iii] title as above, title page in
brick red with lettering in white relief and profile
in white relief and black; verso Copyright 1944
By The World Publishing Company / Manufactured
In The United States Of America; p. [1] Acknowledgments, followed by six lines; verso blank;
pp. [3-6] Contents; pp. 7-13 A Lowbrow Introduction, signed Louis Greenfield / May 1944; p. [14]
blank; pp. 15-17 A Letter to the Editor / from /
Christopher Morley, signed Christopher Morley;
p. [18] blank; p. [19] second fly title Complete
Novels; p. [20] blank; pp. 21-636 text. One blank
leaf at front, one at back.

All-rag wove paper, watermarked Archer / W & A,
with figure of archer. Top edges trimmed and
gilt. Bottom edges trimmed, front edges untrimmed. Bound in brick red cloth, boxed. Front
reads in narrow black panel running to front edge,
in gold, Morley's Variety. Backbone reads, at top,

in gold, Edited by / Louis Greenfield; at bottom, The World / Publishing Company. A long narrow black panel in the center of the backbone reads down, in gold, Morley's Variety. The jacket is semi-transparent paper, without lettering. Box is covered with black paper with brick red panel on front reading in white relief Morley's Variety, followed by profile sketch of Morley in black and white relief.

The first printing appeared November 4, 1944. The note in the introduction of the trade edition about "Soft Shoulders" is deleted in the limited edition.

ANOTHER LETTER TO LORD CHESTERFIELD
1945

Another Letter / To Lord / Chesterfield. / [ornament] / From Samuel Johnson / And Christopher Morley. / First Edition / [row of ornaments] / New-York: / Printed For Ben Abramson / At The Argus Bookshop, 3 West 46Th Street. / M CM XLV

COLLATION: 16mo. Pp. [1-2]-3-6, consisting of p. [1] title as above; verso Copyright, 1945, by Christopher Morley; pp. 3-6 text, opening with row of ornaments and salutation To Lord / Chesterfield, signed Sam. Johnson / (per Christopher Morley). Text printed in 18th century type by William Rudge & Sons. One blank leaf at back.

Wove paper, no watermark. Front edges untrimmed, other edges trimmed. Bound in heavy double brown paper wrappers. Front has, in black, silhouette profile of Samuel Johnson, beneath which reads Another / Letter To Lord / Chesterfield / M CM XLV

The first printing consisted of 1000 copies and appeared July 19, 1945. Reprinted from the "Saturday Review of Literature" February 10, 1945.

ANOTHER LETTER TO LORD CHESTERFIELD
1945
LIMITED EDITION, SIGNED
Collation same as the regular edition, except as
follows: There are an additional fly-leaf at the
front and one at back; recto of fly leaf at the front
has handwritten ink Autographed Edition / Limited
to 200 Copies / This is   ; the title page is autographed by the author; the double wrappers are
replaced by brown boards; there is an onionskin
dust jacket.
   200 copies of the first printing of the regular
edition were issued in the limited edition. Actually 85 of these were autographed by the author
as of September 23, 1948.

SPIRIT LEVEL
1946
Spirit Level / And Other Poems / By / Chris-
topher Morley / [publisher's device] / Harvard
University Press / Cambridge, Massachusetts /
1946
COLLATION: 12mo. Pp. [i-iv]-v-[vi]-vii-[viii]-
ix-x + [1-2]-3-52, consisting of p. [i] fly title
Spirit Level; verso London: Geoffrey Cumberlege /
Oxford University Press; p. [iii] title as above;
verso Copyright, 1946 / By The President and
Fellows Of Harvard College / Printed In The
United States Of America / The Merrymount
Press, Boston; p. v Dedicated / In respect of
twenty years / To Harry Scherman / and Meredith
Wood, followed by two-stanza poem, eight lines;
verso blank; p. vii Acknowledgment, followed by
six lines; verso blank; pp. ix-x Contents; p. [1]
second fly title Spirit Level / and other poems;
verso blank; pp. 3-52 text. One blank leaf at back.

Laid paper, watermarked Flemish Book / Made
In U.S.A. Top edges trimmed, other edges untrimmed. Bound in heavy black cloth. Backbone

reads, in gold, [double rule] / Morley, followed by, reading down, Spirit Level / Harvard / [double rule] .

The jacket is white, overprinted in aquamarine, with a small black figure design. Front reads in white panel with double black box rule Spirit Level / And Other Poems / Christopher Morley / Harvard University Press. Back shows a picture of Christopher Morley reproduced from a portrait painting by Joseph Hirsch. Backstrip reads in white panel same as backbone. Front flap, reader for the book; back flap an advertisement of "Herman Melville," published by Harvard.
  The first printing appeared November 15, 1946, and consisted of 1500 copies.

THE OLD MANDARIN
        1947
Mandarin / More Translations From The Chinese / by Christopher Morley / With Illustrations by Carl Rose / [sketch of a mandarin] / "So you won't need to cancel / The thoughts that you really / think, / Use less indelible pencil / And more invisible ink." / Harcourt, Brace And Company 1947
COLLATION: 12mo. One hundred and twenty-six unnumbered pages, consisting of p. [i] fly title The Old Mandarin; verso The Old / [sketch of two mandarins]; p. [iii] title as above, with the first words in the title The Old appearing on the verso of the fly title; verso six lines of copyright and printing notices and the line first edition; p. [v] Logan Pearsall Smith / 1865-1946, followed by four line poem; verso blank; p. [vii] acknowledgments to publishers for permission to reprint and additional bibliographical information, in all 21 lines, signed C. M. / Roslyn Heights, L. I. / November, 1946; verso blank; pp. [ix-xi] Index Of First Lines; verso [sketch of a mandarin];

pp. [1-113] text; p. [114] blank. One blank leaf at back.

Wove paper, unwatermarked. All edges trimmed. Bound in black cloth. Blind stamped on front are three mandarin figures, on back four mandarin figures. Backbone reads down, in gold, Christopher Morley The Old Mandarin Harcourt, Brace And Company

The jacket is white, overprinted in red. Front has three mandarin figures outlined in black and reads, in white relief, The Old / Mandarin / More Translations From The Chinese / Christopher Morley. Back has four mandarin figures in black outline. Backstrip reads, in white relief, same as backbone. Front flap has review notice of the book, back flap an advertisement for "The Middle Kingdom."
The first printing, 5,000 copies, appeared May 19, 1947.

PARNASSUS ON WHEELS AND THE HAUNTED BOOKSHOP
1948
Parnassus On / Wheels & / The Haunted / Bookshop′ / [rule] / Two Classics in One Volume by / Christopher Morley / Introduction by Joseph A. Margolies / [rule] / Doubleday & Company, Inc. 1948 / Garden City, New York
COLLATION: 8vo. Pp. [i-viii]-ix-xii-[xiii-xvi]-xvii-xviii + [1]-[298], consisting of p. [i] fly title Parnassus On Wheels & / The Haunted Bookshop; verso blank; p. [iii] by Christopher Morley, followed by a list of thirteen titles; verso blank; p. [v] title as above, the whole in a double rule box; verso Copyright, 1917, 1923, 1945, 1946, 1948. By Christopher Morley / All Rights Reserved. Printed In The United States At / The Country Life Press, Garden City, N.Y. First

Edition; p. [vii] Contents, followed by three lines; verso blank; pp. ix-xii Introduction, signed Joseph A. Margolies; p. [xiii] second fly title Parnassus On / Wheels′ /, the whole in a double rule box; verso blank; p. [xiv] To H.B.F. and H.F.M. / "Trusty, dusky, vivid true"; verso blank; pp. xvii-xviii A Letter to David Grayson, Esq., / of Hempfield, U.S.A., signed Faithfully yours, / Christopher Morley.; pp. 1-106 text of Parnassus; p. [107] third fly title The Haunted / Bookshop′ /, the whole in a double rule box; verso To the Booksellers, a dedication signed Christopher Morley. / Philadelphia, April 28, 1919.; p. [109] Contents; verso blank; pp. [111]-296 text of The Haunted Bookshop; p. [297] The Bookstore, followed by twenty-one lines; verso blank. One blank leaf at front, one at back. Rust end papers.

Wove paper, no watermark. Top and bottom edges trimmed, top stained rust, front edges untrimmed. Bound in black cloth, backbone reading, in gold double rule box, Parnassus / On Wheels / & The / Haunted / Bookshop / [rule] / Christopher / Morley / Doubleday′

The jacket is white overprinted in yellow, light yellow, and rust on front and backstrip. Front, top, reads Parnassus / On Wheels / [sketch of bookwagon], on yellow enclosed by broken chain box rule; center, Christopher / Morley / [sketch of leaf], author's name in rust; bottom The Haunted / Bookshop / [sketch of stairway] / Two Classics In One Volume, on rust enclosed by broken chain box rule. Backstrip reads [fancy chain rule] / Parnassus / On / Wheels / [chain rule] / The / Haunted / Bookshop / [chain rule] / Christopher / Morley / [chain rule] / Doubleday / [chain rule]. Back reprints On The Return Of A Book / Lent To A Friend, enclosed in double box rule, in rust. Front flap has photo portrait of

Morley taken of a painting by Joseph Hirsch, followed by reader for this volume which extends over to the back flap.
3000 copies of the first printing appeared January, 1948.

THE MAN WHO MADE FRIENDS WITH HIMSELF
1949
Christopher Morley / The Man / Who / Made / Friends / With / Himself / A Novel / Doubleday & Company, Inc., Garden City, New York, 1949
COLLATION: 8vo. Pp. [i-iv]-v-[vi]-vii-viii-[ix-x] + 1-275-[276], consisting of p. [i] fly title, [ornament] / The Man Who Made / Friends With Himself; verso blank, p. [iii] title as above; verso ten lines of copyright, author's comment on characters and incidents in the book, and printing notices and line First Edition; p. v From Richard Tolman's Musette Bag, followed by twenty lines of quotations; verso blank; p. vii-viii Contents; p. [ix] second fly title [ornament] / The Man Who Made / Friends With Himself; verso blank; pp. 1-275 text; p. [276] blank. One fly leaf at back. Blue end papers.

Laid paper, unwatermarked. Top and bottom edges trimmed, front edges untrimmed. Top edges stained blue. Bound in black cloth, front reading, in gold, autograph signature, Christopher Morley. Backbone has a blue panel reading, in gold, Christopher / Morley / [black rule] / The Man / Who / Made / Friends / With / Himself / [black rule] / Doubleday

The jacket is white overprinted in blue gray with decorations in black and gray. Front reads, in yellow, above gray ornamental border, The / Man Who / Made / Friends / With / Himself. Below gray ornamental border, front reads, in black, A novel by, followed in white relief Christopher

Morley. Above gray ornamental border, back has
a photo portrait of Morley by Lotte Jacobi; below
the border is Morley's autograph signature in
white relief. Above gray ornamental border,
backstrip reads, in yellow, The / Man / Who /
Made / Friends / With / Himself / [in white re-
lief] by / Christopher / Morley / [in yellow]
Doubleday. Flaps are white. Front flap has a
reader for the book; back flap reads Space for the
reader: — / [at bottom] Printed in the U.S.A.
    The regular edition was published June 13, 1949
    in a first printing of 35,000 copies. Sixteen
    hundred copies of a "private edition" were pub-
    lished April 18, 1949, for booksellers. This
    edition differs from the trade edition in three
    particulars: (1) the front cover has a three
    quarter cream paper binding, the paper part
    representing a facsimile manuscript page with
    Morley handwritten corrections in the margin;
    (2) the verso of the first fly title reads [orna-
    ment] Memo / For This Private Edition, fol-
    lowed by twenty three lines, signed Yours,
    theirs, ours, in all respect, / C. M. / February
    17, 1949; (3) the verso of the title page has added
    to the information in the regular edition the line
    Presentation Edition, Not For Sale, and deleted
    the line First Edition.

THE IRONING BOARD
            1949
The Ironing / Board / Christopher Morley / 1949 /
Doubleday & Company, Inc., Garden City, N. Y.
COLLATION: 8vo. Pp. [1-6]-7-8-[9-10]-11-255-
[256], consisting of p. [1] fly title The Ironing
Board; verso blank; p. [3] title as above; verso
Copyright, 1949, By Christopher Morley / All
Rights Reserved / Printed In The United States /
At The Country Life Press, Garden City, N. Y. /
First Edition; p. [5] sixteen lines of dedication;
verso blank; pp. 7-8 Contents; p. [9] second fly

title The Ironing Board; verso blank; pp. 11-255
text; p. [256] blank. No fly leaves.

Laid paper, no watermark. Top edges trimmed
and stained orange; bottom edges trimmed and
other edges untrimmed. Bound in black cloth.
Backbone reads in orange The / Ironing / Board /
[rule] / Christopher / Morley / [rule] / Doubleday,
the whole in orange double rule box.

The jacket is white. Front reads Christopher
Morley / in reddish orange The / Ironing /
Board / [sketch in black] / Morley's own selection
of favorite essays / written in fun and fury over
the last ten years. Back has a portrait of Morley
by Lotte Jacobi and reads Christopher / Morley,
in reddish orange, followed by, in black Contents
From The Ironing Board / eleven lines of Contents
titles in reddish orange rule box / Printed in the
U. S. A. Backstrip reads down Christopher Morley, in reddish orange The Ironing Board, at
bottom Doubleday. Front flap has a reader for the
book; back flap has a note about The Man Who
Made Friends With Himself.
　　Published November 10, 1949, with a first printing of 3500 copies.

POETRY PACKAGE
　　　　1950
Poetry Package / By W.R.B. and C.M. / Introduction by Cuckoo / [sketch, signed by artist Lloyd
Coe] / "Sat est scripsisse." / "Was written by
its Author, who gave it to his Friend." / —Austin
Dobson to Edmund Gosse / Louis Greenfield /
51 East 10th Street / New York 3
COLLATION: 8vo. Pp. [1-46], consisting of p. [1]
fly title Poetry Package; verso blank; p. [3] title
as above, in border of two rules with ornamental
corners; verso Copyright 1950 / by W.R.B. and
C.M.; pp. [5-6] preface Before Opening The

Package signed Cuckoo. / 1949; p. [7] Table Of
Contents; verso blank; pp. [9-39] text; pp. [40-42]
blank; p. [43] Acknowledgement; verso blank;
p. [45] Colophon; verso blank. One blank leaf at
back.

Laid paper, watermarked [figure of eagle] /
Eagle-A / Quality Text / U.S.A. All edges
trimmed. Bound (stapled) in a heavy manila, in
pale yellow, without lettering.

The jacket consists of a heavy, rose paper
wrapper, with lettering and border identical with
the title page except the last three lines are
omitted.
    Contributions by Christopher Morley are listed
in the Table of Contents with the initials D.D.
following the title. The first printing, January
1, 1950, consisted of 1000 copies

A PRIDE OF SONNETS
          1951
A / Pride / Of / Sonnets / Together with / An
Essay on A Sonnet / By / Christopher Morley /
[publisher's device] / [double rule] / Madison
New Jersey / Printed at The Golden Hind Press /
M C M L I
COLLATION: La. 8vo. Pp. [i-iv]-[1-4]-5-[31],
consisting of p. [i] fly title A Pride Of Sonnets;
verso blank; p. [iii] ten-line quotation, followed by
credit line From Strutt's English Sports and
Pastimes, 1800; verso blank; p. [1] title as above,
the publisher's device in red; verso Acknowledgment of Copyright as follows:, followed by sixteen lines of copyright and acknowledgment notices; p. [3] half-title A Sonnet; verso blank; pp. 5-
30 text; p. [31] printing notice in red reads [or-
nament] / Hand set in Weiss Antiqua by Arthur
and Edna / Rushmore, and 250 copies printed on
a hand press / on White Archer paper, at the

Golden Hind Press / in Madison, New Jersey,
November, 1951. One blank page at front, one
at back.

Wove paper, no watermark. Top and front edges
trimmed; bottom edges untrimmed. Bound in
fancy wrappers with marbleized design. Front
has a light tan label with ornamental border, title
in brown reading A / Pride / Of / Sonnets / Together with / An Essay on A Sonnet / By / Christopher Morley
    250 copies printed at the Golden Hind Press,
    Madison, N.J., November, 1951. Sonnets are
    reprinted from works noted in the copyright
    notice.

II. EPHEMERAL PUBLICATIONS

Ephemeral publications are listed alphabetically
by title. Each title is described in a brief note
unless previously listed in the Lee bibliography.
Titles from Lee are followed by page references
(in parentheses) to Lee without further description
unless a correction is noted.

A. EDWARD NEWTON'S CHRISTMAS CARD FOR
1918 (249)

"ALL QUIET ON THE WESTERN FRONT": [AD-
VANCE COMMENT] (249)

AN APOLOGY, AN EXPLANATION, AND AN
APPEAL.—An undated mimeographed announcement from the Argus Book Shop, Chicago, Ill.,
signed Ben Abramson, stating that Morley has de-
cided not to sign copies of "Kitty Foyle." Argus
had sent out an earlier announcement saying Morley would inscribe copies.

AN APPRECIATION OF THUNDER ON THE
LEFT (249)

THE ARGUS BOOK FAIR.— A cream leaflet,
French-fold, 4 9/16" x 6 1/8", sketch of Morley
surrounded by books below title as above, followed
by name of the artist and the lines Christopher
Morley / Master Of Ceremonies. The book fair
announcement of the Argus Book Shop, Inc., 16
North Michigan Avenue, Chicago, Illinois, appears
on the inside. Printed December, 1941.

"THE ARRIVAL OF WILHELM" (249)

THE AUTHOR TO THE PRINTER.— A reprint of
an advertisement which appeared in the "Saturday
Review of Literature," October 9, 1937. A line
at the top reads "This is a letter recently received from Christopher Morley." Reprint is on

cream paper on a single page. Following text is the subscript American Book Bindery, Stratford Press, Inc.

AUTOGRAPHING.— Two items. (1) Copy of a letter by Christopher Morley to Ben Abramson, Argus Book Shop, Chicago, reproduced in blue on Argus Book Shop stationery. No date. (2) Facsimile greeting card, entitled "This Book Belongs To . . . ," 6 1/4" x 4", signed Christopher Morley, April MCMXXXIII. Deals with autographing of books for customers of Katharine Glover's book shop, Los Angeles.

BALLADE OF THE DAY'S RUN (249)

BEN ABRAMSON'S ARGUS BOOK SHOP CATALOG 27.— This catalogue, issued in December 1947, contains a picture of Morley on the cover and a note about him by Ben Abramson (page 35), together with a quotation from "Passivity Program" (pages 35-36).

BLANKET TO COVER A SET OF SHEETS.— Poem with facsimile autograph signature of Christopher Morley written for a sale catalogue issued by Ben Abramson's Argus Book Shop. The four-stanza poem carries the sub-title "Prolegomenon To A Pack of Sybilline Leaves From Argus" and precedes a loose-leaf catalogue of 35 pages issued in October, 1938.

A BOOK OF VERSE OF THE GREAT WAR (249)

BOOKS AND BIDDERS—THE ADVENTURES OF
    A BIBLIOPHILE (250)

A BOOKSELLERS' AUTHOR (250)

BOOKS FOR AUTUMN · 1937. J. B. LIPPIN-
COTT COMPANY.— The new summer and
autumn book catalogue, 1937, Lippincott, contains
on pp. [iii-iv] an essay by Morley entitled "Bib-
liodisia," a brief pen portrait of the founder of
Lippincott's reprinted from "Trade Winds,"
"Saturday Review of Literature," July 3, 1937.
The catalogue contains several announcements
of Morley's books appearing under the Lippincott
imprint and a picture of Morley, along with several
other Lippincott authors, on the front and back
covers.

THE BROWN OWL (250)

BUREAU OF LITERARY CONTROL (250)

CAPTAIN MACEDOINE COCKTAIL (250)

CARGOES FOR CRUSOES (251)

CARL AND ALDA VITZ'S CHRISTMAS CARD
FOR 1940.— Excerpt from "Friends, Ro-
mans . . ." printed on cream, French-fold laid
paper. Issued Christmas 1940 by Carl and Alda
Vitz. Initial letter of excerpt is printed in brown.
Four pages, measuring 6 1/4" x 4 1/2".

CASUALS OF THE SEA, MODERN LIBRARY EDI-
TION (251)

CATALOGUE OF THE THEATRE (251)

CHECKLISTS OF TWENTIETH CENTURY AU-
THORS, SECOND SERIES (251)

THE CHILD AND THE BOOK (251)

CHRISTMAS CARD.— Christopher Morley's 1941
Christmas card, 5 3/8" x 3 3/4", French-fold
watermarked paper, was printed by William E.

Rudge's Sons, New York. The front bears the
legend "Even thinking about / God is no excuse
for keeping / Other people Out of the / Bathroom,
— C.M. / First Edition.

CHRISTMAS CARDS (251)

THE CHRISTOPHER MORLEY INN.— A blotter,
white glazed in front, blue back, 2 1/4" x 3 1/2".
Sketch of waitress upper left; Lombard 2892 /
The Christopher Morley / Inn / 704 So. Washington Square / We Satisfy Your Appetite and Econo-
mize on Your Purse. Try us. / Luncheon 11-12
French Pastry. There were several other issues
of these blotters.

CHRISTOPHER MORLEY JOINS THE KNOX
FAMILY.— A one-page account of Morley serving
as lecturer on the William L. Honnold Foundation
lecture series in the Spring of 1938. The account,
illustrated with a picture of Morley and Canby and
another of Morley and students, appears in a Knox
College brochure entitled People / The Important / Thing At Knox [n.d.]. It contains a quotation
from a letter of Morley to Knox students. The
series of lectures was entitled "Literature As
Companionship."

CHRISTOPHER MORLEY'S SCRAPBOOK (252)

THE CONCORD EDITION OF THE WORKS OF
    JOSEPH CONRAD (252)

CONTEMPORARY WAR POEMS (252)

CRONYN & LOWNDES GALLERIES (252)

DAUBER AND PINE CATALOGUE ONE HUNDRED.
— A 48 page pamphlet bound in brick colored,
heavy paper wrappers. Published by the Dauber

and Pine Bookshops, Inc., December 1931. Page 14 contains a testimonial by Morley which was also published in a collection of the testimonials appearing in this Catalogue printed as a separate under the title "Opinions On The Amenities of Book-Collecting" (q.v.).

DAWSON'S BOOK SHOP CATALOGUE 91 (253)

DEDICATION FOR A BOOKSELLER'S WINDOW. — By Christopher Morley. A four-page leaflet, 9 1/4" x 6 1/4", consisting of six verses by Morley, an announcement of the opening of Kroch's enlarged bookstore November 19, 1937, and a list of different types of stock (e.g. stationery) sold by Kroch in addition to books.

EDDIE NEWTON'S RIDE (253)

EDITORIAL ROOM BROADSIDE (253)

THE EIGHTH SIN: [ARTICLE ABOUT] (253)

THE EQUITABLE TRUST COMPANY OF AT-LANTIC CITY (253)

EXHIBITION WOOD AND LINOLEUM ENGRAV-INGS. — A four-page leaflet, 6 1/4" x 3 1/2", announcing an exhibition of Henry R. Diamond's engravings, October 8-20, 1934, by Duttons Inc. Pages [2-3] contain a letter of appreciation of the work of Henry Diamond by Christopher Morley, with facsimile autograph signature.

50TH ANNIVERSARY COLUMBIA UNIVERSITY PRESS FALL BOOKS. — This catalogue, issued in the Fall of 1943, contains on page [1] "The Watchman's Sonnet," a poem composed on the occasion of the Fiftieth Anniversary of Columbia University Press by the Press's Honorary Night

Watchman, with autograph signature Christopher Morley. Copyright, 1943, Columbia University Press.

A FRAGMENT FROM DONNE (253-254)

GELBER · LILIENTHAL · INC. (254)

GENTHE PHOTOGRAPHS OF GREECE (254)

GEOFFREY CHAUCER.— A Rosenbach Company catalogue entitled "An Exhibition of Fifteenth Century Manuscripts and Books in Honor of the Six Hundredth Anniversary of the Birth of Geoffrey Chaucer (1340-1400), March 25 to April 30, 1940 at the Rosenbach Company, 15 East 51st Street, New York City. On page [3] appears the poem "Ballade Of An Old Friend," signed Christopher Morley. The catalogue of the exhibit contains sixteen pages, 9 1/4" x 6", and two illustrations from the "Canterbury Tales" manuscripts.

GETTING RID OF BILL (254)

GOTHAM BOOK MART CATALOG 37.— The Morley contribution consists of a paragraph on the cover page reprinted from the "Saturday Review of Literature." The catalogue consists of 84 pages, 1055 numbered items, and measures 8" x 5 1/4". Published in the Spring of 1937.

HARD LINES.— A yellow card, 6 1/2" x 10 1/2", green border, green box and rule, printed in violet: Christopher Morley says of / Hard / Lines / [rule] / It's grand comedy— / I think it precisely clicks / with the wave-length of 1931.

HAVE YOU READ "CASUALS OF THE SEA"? (254)

HEYWOOD. — By Christopher Morley. A leaflet of four pages (9" x 6") issued by the Book-Of-The-Month Club. The first page, entitled "In Memoriam," is a picture of Heywood Broun. Page 3 carries the first appearance of a one-page article by Christopher Morley entitled "Heywood."

HOBOKEN FREE STATE. — · Hoboken Free State · / E Pluribus Euthanasia in form of seal, with emblem of Three-Hours-for-Lunch Club in centre / Authorized Consulate / [double rule] / Hoboken / Free / State / E Pluribus Euthanasia
  This membership certificate is printed on a yellow card, watermarked Bodleian. An embossed yellow seal, reading same as above, is gummed to the lower left corner.

HYMN TO THE DAIRYMAIDS ON BEACON
  STREET (254)

IMPROMPTU POEM FOR BEN ABRAMSON. — A four-line poem, printed on rough, buff cardboard 6 3/8" x 4 1/8", dated February 24, 1933. The verso of the card reads One hundred copies of this first print- / ing were done for the occasion of a / reception to their friends by Christo- / pher Morley and The Argus Book / Shop. November 13, 1937. This is / Number Three-hundred-thirty-three.

IN AN AUCTION ROOM (255)
  Lee p. 255, line 10: Change words "The Rocking Horse" to "Hide and Seek."

"IN SMALL PROPORTIONS WE JUST BEAUTIES
  SEE" (255)

JEMIMA PLAYS HER SOFT GUITAR (255)

A JOHN MISTLETOE CALENDAR. — A

14 1/2" x 9 3/4" calendar printed on stiff card-board. The title is followed by the descriptive phrase "A delightful companion for an hour, a day, or a year," credited to Donald Gordon of the American News. The calendar contains a quotation for each month from "John Mistletoe" and is printed in black and green on yellow. Published by Doubleday, Doran & Co., Inc., undated.

JOURNALIZATION OF THOUGHT, THE (255-256)
Lee p. 256, line 1: Insert opening quotation before word "Book-" and delete period after word "Club," inserting word "News," closing with quotation marks and a period.

JURGEN AND THE CENSOR (256)

KROCH'S BOOKSTORES, INC. (256)

THE LAND OF PERPETUAL YOUTH (256)

A LETTER FROM CHRISTOPHER MORLEY.— A four-page mimeographed letter telling reviewers about F. V. Morley's "My One Contribution To Chess." The letter is addressed to "Dear Doris" and is dated October 10, 1945.

LITERARY LIGHTS (256)

A LITTLE LITERATURE WITH YOUR READING (256)

A MAGNIFICENT FARCE, AND OTHER DIVERSIONS OF A BOOK-COLLECTOR (257)

MEMORIAL EDITION OF JOSEPH CONRAD'S COLLECTED WORKS (257)

A MESSAGE FOR VINCENT STARRETT.— A four-page leaflet, 7" x 5", published in 1942 by

Edwin B. Hill at Ysleta, Texas. Thirty copies
were printed. The text appears on pages [2-3]
and is signed Christopher Morley / (April 24,
1942). Page [4] reads The Annual Literary Award
of the Friends of Litera- / ture was given to Mr.
Starrett, on May 9, 1942, at a / dinner of the
Chicago Foundation for Literature, / Dr. Preston
Bradley presiding as Master of Cere- / monies.
After the award, and Mr. Starrett's response, /
Dr. Bradley read the foregoing "message" from /
Christopher Morley, a few copies of which are
now / privately printed for the satisfaction of
friends of both / writers and of all concerned.

MORRELL HOUSEHOLD CALENDAR FOR 1936
(257)
Lee p. 257, line 5: Insert after word "colors,":
This appeared also in a larger format,
30" x 14".

THE MOSHER BOOK CATALOGUE (257)

NEW YORK HERALD TRIBUNE ADVERTISE-
MENT.— A letter from Morley to the Advertising
Manager of the New York Herald Tribune which
speaks of the effectiveness of an advertisement
in the Herald Tribune for "The Trojan Horse"
which was then playing at the Millpond Playhouse,
Roslyn, L. I. The letter is dated November 6,
1940, and carries Morley's autograph signature.
Below is printed the reply from the New York
Herald Tribune. Both letters are reproduced on
a single white page 8" x 11". A portion of the
page is overprinted in yellow.

ON MINDING OUR MANNERS IN SPEECH (257)

AN OPEN LETTER FROM CHRISTOPHER MOR-
LEY.— An eight-page leaflet, 6" x 4 1/2",
printed in green on green paper with a woodcut

illustration of Morley on the cover. It consists of a letter to President Paul D. Eddy of Adelphi College from Morley, dated April 1, 1939, printed as a tribute to the College in the "Adelphi College Bulletin" vol. iii, No. 8, April, 1939, Adelphi College, Garden City, New York.

OPINIONS ON THE AMENITIES OF BOOK-COLLECTING. — As Expressed By A Group Of Seasoned Bibliophiles On The Occasion Of The Printing of Catalogue One Hundred. The Morley contribution consists of a letter of ten lines on page [9], signed Christopher Morley. The leaflet, measuring 7" x 6", contains sixteen unnumbered pages of testimonials.

AN OUTLINE OF DISTINGUISHED READING (257-258)

PARNASSUS ON WHEELS, MODERN LIBRARY EDITION (258)

PATRIOTIC PIECES FROM THE GREAT WAR (258)

THE PHARISEES. — By M. Morgan Gibbon. Garden City and Toronto (Doubleday, Page & Co.), 1922. The front of the jacket contains a twenty-line comment by Morley about Miss Gibbon's authorship. The front flap contains a note by Morley about Don Marquis's book, "Poems and Portraits."

PHILIP C. DUSCHNES CATALOGUE 29. — First editions of esteemed American and British authors; fine Doves, Kelmscott, Ashendene, Limited Editions Club, Bruce Rogers, and other Press books. A four stanza poem, signed P.E.G. Quercus and entitled "Dibbies On It First (Or, the Alpha and Omega of Book Collecting)," appears on the

front cover. The Catalogue contains 60 pages and
857 numbered titles for sale and measures
10" x 7". It contains no date but reads on verso
of cover "Certain new books of 1938 are listed
herein before publication." One verse from the
poem also appeared on List #626 (mimeographed)
of the Argus Book Shop, Inc.

POEMS ABOUT GOD (258)

PROOFREADERS'S MIND. — No. XIII in the series
of Typophile Monographs. A leaflet of four pages
measuring 4 1/2" x 7", on gray laid paper. Title
on cover. Page 2 is blank. Page 3 has decorative
typographic panels 1 1/2 inches in height printed
in blue and black on bottom, between them the
poem "Proofreader's Mind" from "Parson's
Pleasure." Colophon in lower right corner of
back cover reads TYPOPHILE MONOGRAPHS:
XIII / Produced by Ted Freedman at / The Platen
Press, Orinda, California. / From Parson's
Pleasure, / Copyright, 1924, by Christopher Morley, / Published by J. B. Lippincott Co. No date
is shown, but the monograph accompanied Typophile Chap Book No. XII, "The Bowker Lectures
on Book Publishing: Second Series," issued in
1945.

REHEARSAL: A COMEDY IN ONE ACT (258)

RIESENBERG'S "THE LOG OF THE SEA." (258)

A ROUND-TABLE IN POICTESME (259)

SARAH BALL BOOK STATIONS (259)

SCARF: THE MAN WHO MADE FRIENDS WITH
HIMSELF. — The jacket designs for "The Man
Who Made Friends With Himself," and other Mor-
ley titles were reproduced on a 36" square silk

scarf by the publisher, Doubleday, for booksellers to use in advertising purposes. The scarf has a three inch yellow border and the jackets are reproduced in a variety of colors within this border, the largest being THE MAN WHO MADE FRIENDS WITH HIMSELF, which is featured as a center piece. The title of this book is printed in black on white around the inner edges of the yellow border of the scarf followed by the signature of Christopher Morley. The scarf was also made available for sale to the public by Louis Greenfield, publisher.

THE SECOND MATE (259)

SHERLOCK HOLMES'S PRAYER. — A four page leaflet, 7" x 4 3/4", copyrighted, 1944, by Christopher Morley, and reading on the first page Sherlock Holmes's / Prayer / Specially printed for / the Sherlock Holmes dinner / of the Baker Street Irregulars, / March 31, 1944 / [rule] / Dr. Watson / edited by Christopher Morley.

SHERLOCKIANA TWO SONNETS. — By Christopher Morley and Vincent Starrett. A four-page leaflet, 7 3/4" x 5", published in 1942 by Edwin B. Hill at Ysleta, Texas. Sixty copies were printed November, 1942. Morley's "Sonnet On Baker Street" appears on page [2] and is signed Christopher Morley / May 4, 1942.

"SMELLS." (259)

SOCK AND BUSKIN. — A four-page leaflet announcing the production of an adaptation of Christopher Morley's "Trojan Horse" by Sock and Buskin, the Brown University Dramatic Society, March 23, 24, 25, 26, 1938.

SOFT SHOULDERS: PLAYBILL. — The playbill

for the Millpond Playhouse performance of Morley's Play "Soft Shoulders," Wednesday thru Saturday, July 17-20, 1940. The playbill appears in the official organ of the Millpond Playhouse, entitled "The Claque," July 15, 1940. The announcement of the cast is preceded by a one-page article "The Claque Quacks," signed Christopher Morley.

SOME SHIPS OF TODAY AND YESTERDAY (259)

THE STORY OF A BELGIAN DOG (259)

THE STUFF AND NONSENSE SCRAP-BOOK, NUMBER 4, DECEMBER 13, 1935.— Contains an article headed "Local Boy Makes Good" with the editor's note: "So far as may be determined at this late date, the following paragraphs represent Mr. Christopher Morley's first appearance in the 'Evening Public Ledger.' They were printed there on March 11, 1918." The Scrap-Book, with verso of cover dedication to Morley, carried the Program of Festivities of the Stuff and Nonsense Dinner, held in Philadelphia, December 13, 1935, at which Christopher Morley was the guest speaker. Actually Morley made his first appearance in the Philadelphia "Evening Public Ledger" March 11, 1918, under the column heading "The Unnatural Naturalist."

THE TAVERN OF THE FOOLS (259-260)
    Lee p. 260, line 1: Change word "American" to "Magazine."

THIS BOOK-COLLECTING GAME (260)

"THREE'S A CROWD" (260)

THUNDER ON THE LEFT (260)

"TICKLED TO DEATH" (260)

TOLMANISMS. — A selection from "The Man Who Made Friends With Himself" by Christopher Morley, compiled by Donald Elder. A pamphlet of twelve pages, 8 1/4" x 5 3/8", published by Doubleday & Company, Inc., Garden City, New York, 1949. Verso of the cover carries four lines of copyright information and the line First Edition.

TO THE CLASS OF 1910: FAIR WARNING. — A folder on buff wove paper, 10 1/2" x 7", published in 1915. The heading above, in italics, constitutes the only introduction. Pages [1] and [3] contain the text, pages [2] and [4] are blank. Signed Christopher Morley. Text closes with fancy tailpiece.

TRADE WINDS (260-261)

TROILUS AND CRESSIDA. — The Monthly Letter of the Limited Editions Club (September 1939, Number 120), in announcing its new title, gives considerable space to Christopher Morley's views of Geoffrey Chaucer and "Troilus and Cressida."

UNION SQUARE BOOK SHOP (261)

WASHING THE DISHES (261)

WHEN WINTER COMES TO MAIN STREET (261)

WHERE THE BLUE BEGINS. — Announcement of play performance of Morley's novel appearing February 21 to March 4, 1939, at the Pasadena Playhouse, Pasadena, Calif. Printed on white and blue leaflet, 11" x 8 1/2", both sides. Morley portrait on one side.

WHERE THE BLUE BEGINS (Airedale Edition) (261)

WHERE THE BLUE BEGINS: PLAYBILL.— The playbill for the opening night (February 21, 1939) of the Pasadena Playhouse performance of "Where The Blue Begins" is an eight-page leaflet measuring 8 1/2" x 5 1/2".

WHISKY (262)

THE YOUTH OF PARNASSUS (262)

III. BOOKS CONTAINING CONTRIBUTIONS
BY CHRISTOPHER MORLEY

Contributions appearing in the Lee bibliography
are listed here by title only, followed by a page
reference to where the collation in Lee may be
found and by the date of the title. In a few instances these title listings are followed by a note
correcting or adding something to the original
collation in Lee. Brief collations are given for
all contributions appearing after the publication of
Lee (1935) as well as for a few earlier titles which
did not appear in Lee.

GREAT CAESAR!
1909
[fancy rule design] / Great Caesar! / Junior
Play / of the / Class of Nineteen Ten / of / Haverford / College / [ornamental rule] / Staton Brothers, / 5402-5404 Germantown Ave. / Philadelphia,
Pa.

Folio. 30 pp. Wove paper. Gray wrappers, green
and gold decoration.
    Christopher Morley (then C.D.) wrote or as-
    sisted in writing the words for three of the
    songs. He was a member of the cast and
    probably co-author of the play. Page 3 carries
    at the bottom the line Copyright 1909 by Staton
    Brothers.

HAVERFORD COLLEGE CLASSBOOK (209)
1910

AMERICAN RHODES SCHOLARS [CLASSBOOK] (209-210)
1913

THE KAISER (210)
1914

PICTURED KNOWLEDGE (210-211)
1919

THE GENTLE ART OF COLUMNING (211)
1920
Lee p. 211, line 10: Change "Yellow cloth" to
"Gray green boards."

BACK TO HAVERFORD AND— (211-212)
[1920]

FOLK SONGS OF MANY PEOPLES
1921-1922
Folk Songs of Many Peoples / With English Ver-
sions by American Poets / Compiled and Edited /
by / Florence Hudson Botsford / Volume One
[or Volume Two] / [ten lines from—Image of a
Mystic.] / x x x x x / The Woman's Press /
600 Lexington Avenue / New York City

4to. Volume One 235 pp., Volume Two 464 pp.
Wove paper.
    Contains the poem "When the Sun Shines," from
the Polish, English version by Morley, v. 1,
page 79. Also, a poem, "The Winds Blow,"
from the Ukranian, paraphrased by Morley,
v. 1, page 115.

DEVOTION
1922
Devotion / Song / Words by / Christopher Mor-
ley / Music by / Richard Hageman / Low Voice
N. Y. 243 <u>High Voice</u> N. Y. 242 / Price 40 cents
net—No Discount / G. Ricordi & Co., / 14 East
43rd Street / New York / And At / London,
Paris, / Rome, Palermo, Naples, / Buenos-Ayres
And Milan. / Printed In U. S. A.

Folio. 10 pp. Wove paper. Unbound sheet music.
    The words are from "Songs For A Little
House" (1917).

EXPLORERS OF THE DAWN (212)
1922

A TREASURY OF PLAYS FOR WOMEN (212-213)
1922

JUSTICE OF THE PEACE (213)
1923

PARODIES ON WALT WHITMAN (213-214)
1923

NINE ANSWERS BY G. BERNARD SHAW (214)
1923

CASUALS OF THE SEA (214-215)
1923
Lee p. 214, line 3: 1923 should read 1922. Line 5,
insert comma at end of line; delete lines 6 and 7,
substituting therefor: N. Y., and Toronto / Doubleday, Page & Company / 1922

RECITATIONS OLD AND NEW FOR BOYS AND
    GIRLS (215)
1924

A DAUGHTER OF THE SAMURAI (215-216)
1925

FULL AND BY (216-217)
1925
De Luxe Edition

THE JESSAMY BRIDE (217)
1926

SERENADE (217)
1926

VIGNETTES OF THE SEA (218)
1926

YEAR BOOK OF THE PENNSYLVANIA SO-
CIETY (218)
1927
Lee p. 218: Insert in line 10, following word
"buckram": There were five large-paper copies,
bound in leather.

AN OLD-FASHIONED CHRISTMAS (219)
1927

THE WRITINGS OF A. EDWARD NEWTON
(219-220)
1927

RUSSELL HILLARD LOINES (220)
1927

THE SEA AND THE JUNGLE (220-221)
1928

SHELFWARD HO! (221)
[1928]

THE BASTABLE CHILDREN (221-222)
1928

THOUGHTS AT THE BOTTOM OF A MUG OF
CIDER (222)
1928

A MAN'S WOMAN (222-223)
1928

MORROW'S ALMANACK FOR 1929 (223-224)
1928

POT SHOTS FROM PEGASUS (224)
1929

A CONRAD MEMORIAL LIBRARY (224-225)
1929

O. HENRY [ENCYCLOPAEDIA BRITANNICA]
(225)
1929

WANDERER'S END (225-226)
1930

THE COMPLETE SHERLOCK HOLMES (226)
1930
Lee p. 226, line 6: Insert after words "Volume
I /" ["or Volume II /"]

THE SHORT STORIES OF SAKI (226)
1930
Also reprinted in Modern Library with Morley
preface pages [v]-vii

THE BOOK OF DILEMMAS (227)
1931

THE ADVENTURES OF TOM SAWYER (227-228)
1931

THE MAIDEN VOYAGE
1931
The / Maiden / Voyage / by / Felix Riesenberg /
& / Archie Binns / New York / The John Day
Company. 12mo. 288 pp.
  Based on the unpublished play "The Second
  Mate" (Lee page 259), by Christopher Morley
  and Felix Riesenberg, the same characters
  being used. The play was presented at the
  Rialto Theatre, Hoboken, March 24, 1930.

THE NEW YORKER SCRAPBOOK (228)
1931

BEST COLLEGE VERSE 1931 (228)
1931

A CHRISTMAS BOOK LIST
1932
A Christmas / Book List / from / [portrait of
Christopher Morley, with signature beneath] /
Personally selected at our request for our patrons

8vo. 24 pp. Wove paper. Heavy wrappers, green,
black and white on the outside, book lists inside.
The Morley article appears on pages 1-3. Issued by Marshall Field & Company, Chicago.

THE MAIDES TRAGEDY (229)
1932

EAT, DRINK & BE MERRY IN MARYLAND
(229-230)
1932

THE STANDARD BOOK OF BRITISH AND AMER-
ICAN VERSE (230)
1932

ENGLAND, THEIR ENGLAND (230)
1933

HAVERFORD COLLEGE CENTENARY (231)
1933

A HISTORY OF AMERICAN GRAPHIC HUMOR
(231)
1933

A BOOK OF GREAT AUTOBIOGRAPHY
1934
A Book Of / Great Autobiography / [rule] / Christopher Morley / Joseph Conrad / Selma Lagerlöf /
Helen Keller / William McFee / W.N.P. Bar-

bellion / Walt Whitman / Itsu Inagaki Sugimoto /
[publisher's device] / [rule] / Doubleday, Doran &
Company, Inc. / Garden City 1934 New York

8vo. Reprinted from original plates, with separate
paging. Wove paper. Black cloth.
Contains Christopher Morley's "The Autogenesis Of A Poet" with the publisher's biographical note on Morley; Morley's introduction
to Sugimoto's "A Daughter Of The Samurai";
and an account of Morley's discovery of William
McFee which appears in the publisher's introduction to McFee's "The Pattern-Makers."

DESIGNED FOR READING (232)
        1934

THE PANORAMA OF MODERN LITERATURE
(232-233)
        1934

THE POCKET UNIVERSITY
        1934
The Pocket University / [rule] / Guide To Daily
Reading / Edited by / William Rose Benét, Litt.
D., / of The Saturday Review of Literature / in
consultation with / Henry Seidel Canby, Litt. D., /
Editor-in-Chief of The Saturday Review of Literature / and Christopher Morley, Litt. D., /
Contributing Editor of The Saturday / Review of
Literature / [ornament] / Volume XIII / [rule] /
Doubleday, Doran & Company, Inc. / New York
1934 12mo. 227 pp.
Morley served as consultant and appears to
have no specific contribution in the volume,
although he is quoted several times in Benét's
preface. The set was reprinted in 1938 and
again in 1941 by the publisher. It was formerly
published under the title "Master Classics."

DREAMTHORP (233)
1934

POST-BAG DIVERSIONS
1934
Post-Bag Diversions / Elicited By / E. V. Lucas /
'Let others do the work.' / Beau Brummell /
With 12 Illustrations / [publisher's device] /
Methuen & Co. Ltd. / 36 Essex Street W. C. /
London 8vo. 256 pp.
 Morley's contributions consist of three letters
 to E. V. Lucas appearing on pages 146-149.

THE SMART SET ANTHOLOGY (233-234)
1934
Lee p. 234: Insert as paragraph following Line 5:
Copies exist with "Roscoe" instead of "Rascoe"
on the backbone.

LINWEAVE LIMITED EDITIONS (234)
1934

THUNDER ON THE LEFT
1934
Thunder On The Left / A Play in Three Acts /
By / Jean Ferguson Black / From the novel of
the same name / By Christopher Morley / Copyright, 1925 (as a novel), by Christopher Morley /
Copyright, 1928, by Jean Ferguson Black / Copyright, 1934, by Jean Ferguson Black / [eleven lines
of copyright notice] / Samuel French, Inc. /
25 West 45th Street, New York, N. Y. / 811 West
7th Street, Los Angeles, Calif. / Samuel French,
Ltd., London / Samuel French (Canada), Ltd.
Toronto 12mo. 112 pp.
 This dramatization of Morley's novel was presented at the Hedgerow Theatre, Rose Valley,
 Pa., on July 27, 1929, and also on October 31,
 1933, at the Maxine Elliott Theatre, New York
 City.

PRIZE AWARDS FOR STUDENT LIBRARIES (235)
[1935]

THE LIFE AND OPINIONS OF TRISTRAM
SHANDY, GENTLEMAN (235)
1935

1935

An Anthology of / Light Verse / Edited And With
An Introduction By / Louis Kronenberger / [pub-
lisher's device] / [rule] / The Modern Library ·
New York / [rule] 12mo. 291 pp.
"The Tryst" appears on pages 215-216.

Barnacles from Many Bottoms / Scraped and
Gathered for / B R / By the Typophiles / 1935
8vo. 218 pp. unnumbered. Frontispiece and
numerous illustrations. Edited by Paul A. Bennett,
who in his preface states there are "twenty-nine
inserts, the result of fifty-six individual contributions . . . among them the work of seven artists,
fifteen writers, and twenty-six printers." Bound
in black cloth, gold decoration.
  Morley's contribution, entitled "BR's Secret
  Passion," appeared also as a separate (Lee
  p. 206).

Bermuda / 8 Reproductions / in Color from /
Paintings / by / Adolph Treidler
La. folio.' 4 pp. Eight reproductions laid in. En-
closed in gray-blue folding case.
  Page 3 of the folio contains a twelve-line letter
  signed in autograph facsimile.

[rule] / The Cat In Verse / Compiled by Carolyn
Wells / and Louella D. Everett / [rule] / [sketch
of three cats] / with Illustrations By Meta
Plückebaum / Boston / 1935 / Little, Brown, And
Company / [rule] 12mo. 289 pp.

97

"In Honor Of Taffy Topaz" appears on page 185;
reprinted from "Songs For A Little House"
(1917).

Essays in / Modern Thought / Collected By /
Thomas R. Cook / [three lines] / [publisher's
device] / D. C. Heath · And · Company / New York
Boston Chicago / Atlanta San Francisco Dallas
London 12mo. 307 pp.
"Alice And The Aquitania" appears on pages
194-204; reprinted from the "Saturday Review
of Literature," November 21, 1931.

The / Le Gallienne / Book Of / English & American Poetry / [ornament] / Edited With Introduction by / Richard Le Gallienne / Two Volumes In
One / Garden City Publishing Co., Inc. / Garden
City / New York 16mo. 968 pp.
"To A Post-Office Inkwell" appears on page
358; reprinted from "The Rocking Horse"
(1919).

A National Forum For The Discussion of Public
Questions / [ornament] / America's / Town Meeting / of the Air / Literature And Life / [orna-
ment] / Broadcast from / The Town Hall, New
York / over Station WJZ and Associated Stations, /
under the Auspices of / The League For Political
Education, Inc. / and the / National Broadcasting
Company / Edited By / Lyman Bryson / Professor of Education, Teachers College / Columbia
University / American Book Company / 88 Lexington Avenue, New York, N. Y. 16mo. 34 pp.
Morley served as leader of this radio sym-
posium, assisted by Fannie Hurst, T. S.
Stribling, Aubrey Wurdemann, and Francis
Talbot. Morley's remarks are scattered
throughout the talks; his opening remarks appear
on pages 6-14.

The Mark Twain Commemoration. Reprinted from
the Columbia University Quarterly, December,
1935.
4to. Entire reprint occupies pp. [357]-378. Laid
paper, watermarked. Unbound.
The Morley contribution "The Return Of
Huckleberry Finn" appears on pages 370-378.

The New Yorker / Book Of Verse / An Anthology /
Of Poems First Published / In The New Yorker /
1925-1935 / Harcourt, Brace And Company / New
York 8vo. 312 pp.
"Epigrams In A Cellar" appears on pages
295-297.

[ornament] / [four rules] / 1935 / Essay Annual /
A Yearly Collection of Signifi- / cant Essays,
Personal, Critical, Controversial, and Humorous /
Erich A. Walter / Department of English, Univer-
sity of Michigan / [ornament] / Scott, Foresman
And Company / Chicago-Atlanta-Dallas-New
York / [four rules] / [ornament] 12mo. 376 pp.
"Old Loopy" appears on pages 71-77; reprinted
from the "Saturday Review of Literature,"
December 8, 1934.

The / Poet's Craft / Verses selected by / Helen
Fern Daringer / & / Anne Thaxter Eaton / [four
lines] / [ornament] / Illustrated by / Helene
Carter / Yonkers-on-Hudson, New York / World
Book Company 8vo. 338 pp.
"Animal Crackers" appears on page 65; re-
printed from "Chimneysmoke" (1921).

Senior English / For Everyday Use / Eleventh
And Twelfth Years / By / Abram Royer
Brubacher, Ph.D., LL.D. / President, State Col-
lege For Teachers / Albany, New York / Katherine
Eleanor Wheeling, A.M. / [three lines] / And /
Mary Osborne Bryant, A.M. / [two lines] / [pub-

lisher's device] / Charles E. Merrill Company /
New York / Chicago 8vo. 681 pp.
  The Morley contribution is a letter to Helen
Fay, dated November 7, 1931, appearing on
pages 123-124.

Sung / Under The / Silver Umbrella / [rule] /
Poems for Young Children / Selected by the /
Literature Committee Of The / Association For
Childhood Education / [sketch of small boy] / Il-
lustrated by Dorothy Lathrop / New York / The
Macmillan Company / 1935 La. 8vo. 211 pp.
  "Animal Crackers" appears on page 28; re-
printed from "Songs For A Little House" (1917).

[ornaments] / So Red The Nose / or / Breath /
in the Afternoon / Edited By Sterling North / And
Carl Kroch / Illustrated By Roy C. Nelson / [or-
nament] / Farrar & Rinehart / Incorporated / On
Murray Hill · New York 12mo. 73 unnumbered
pages.
  Morley's contribution appears on page [31] and
is entitled "Christopher Morley's Swiss Family
Manhattan Cocktail," faced by a caricature on
page [30].

1936

Anthology Of / Magazine Verse / for 1935 / And
Yearbook Of / American Poetry / Edited by /
Alan F. Pater / New York / The Poetry Digest
Association / MCMXXXVI 12mo. 148 pp.
  "Rubaiyat Of Account Overdue" appears on
page 118. Reprinted from the "Saturday Re-
view of Literature" April 20, 1935; also ap-
peared as a separate (q.v.).

The Complete / Sherlock Holmes / By A. Conan
Doyle / With a Preface by / Christopher Morley /
[publisher's device] / [rule] Doubleday, Doran &

Company, Inc. / Garden City, New York / 1936
8vo. 1340 pp.
A complete reset of the two-volume Memorial
Edition (Lee, page 226). The Morley introduction, "In Memoriam, Sherlock Holmes" appears
on pages vii-xi. The one-volume edition was
issued September 4, 1936, in an edition of 10,000
copies. On August 1, 1938, the book, with
slightly altered title page, was reprinted by the
Garden City Publishing Company.

The Complete Works of / William Shakespeare /
The Cambridge Edition Text, as edited by /
William Aldis Wright / Including the Temple
Notes / Illustrated by / Rockwell Kent / With a
Preface by / Christopher Morley / [ornament] /
Garden City Publishing Company, Inc. / Garden
City MCMXXXVI New York 4to. 1527 pp.
The Morley preface, entitled "A Letter to A
Reader," appears on pages ix-xviii and is signed
in autograph facsimile, dated July, 1936. Re-
printed in 1946 under imprint of the Blakiston
Company.

The Complete Works of / William Shakespeare /
The Cambridge Edition Text, as edited by /
William Aldis Wright / Including the Temple
Notes / Illustrated by / Rockwell Kent / With a
Preface by / Christopher Morley / [ornament] /
Volume I / Doubleday, Doran & Company, Inc. /
Garden City MCMXXXVI New York Folio.
Volumes I and II, 1528 pp.
The Morley preface, entitled "A Letter To A
Reader," appears on pages ix-xviii of Volume I.
It is signed in autograph facsimile and dated
July 1936. Edition limited to 750 numbered
copies, signed by the artist. Enclosed in heavy
board slipcase.

Diggings / from many ampersandhogs / The
Typophiles [vertical, running up] [illustration]
Christmas 1936 [vertical, running down]

16mo. 346 pp., mostly unnumbered. Numerous
illustrations. Made up from thirty-five signa-
tures, with three inserts, from as many authors
and presses. Edited by Paul A. Bennett. Bound
in brown boards and enclosed in slipcase.
  The Morley signature is entitled "The Apologia
of the Ampersand" which also appeared as a
separate (q.v.). A four-line quotation from the
"Bowling Green" appears on page [3].

Letters / of / Rudyard Kipling / With an Introduction by / Christopher Morley / [fancy rule] /
Privately Printed / Christmas, 1936, 12mo.
42 pp.
  The Morley introduction, in epistolary form,
is on pages 5-11. Page [41] states: This edition
is limited to seventy-five copies for presentation / and has been printed by The Southworth-
Anthoensen Press, / Portland, Maine, December, 1936. / Number

New York / World's Fair / 1939 / [dash] / New
York / MCMXXXVI Elephant folio. 32 pp. Heavy
wove paper. Blue leather. In fancy waxed wrapper
and box printed in colors. Beautifully illustrated.
  A prospectus for the World's Fair to which
Morley contributed the essay "Principality And
Power," pages [27-31]. In abbreviated form it
appeared in the "Saturday Review of Litera-
ture" June 26, 1937, under the heading "New
York, One Way."

[rule] / Prose, Poetry and Drama / for Oral Interpretation; / Second Series / Selected and
Arranged by / William J. Farma / [three lines] /
[ornament] / Harper & Brothers Publishers / New

York and London / 1936 / [rule] 8vo. 529 pp.·
"Bivalves" appears on page 157; reprinted
from "Translations From The Chinese" (1922).
"The World's Most Famous Oration" appears
on page 371; reprinted from "Pipefuls" (1920).
"Essayage" appears on pages 414-416; reprinted from the "New Yorker," July 21, 1928.

Selected Poems / Of / T. A. Daly / including
songs from / Mc Aroni Ballads / Canzoni & Songs
Of Wedlock / Madrigal: / Carmina / Mc Aroni
Medleys / With an introductory letter by / Chris-
topher Morley / Harcourt, Brace And Company /
New York 8vo. 273 pp.
    The introductory letter by Christopher Morley
    is printed on pages vii-ix, entitled "A Letter
    To The Publishers." 2600 copies were issued
    August 27, 1936.

Sale Number 4251 / Exhibition Daily From April
11 / Weekdays 9 to 6 Sunday 2 to 5 / Manuscripts,
Autograph Letters / First Editions and Portraits
of / Walt Whitman / Formerly the Property of the
Late / Dr. Richard Maurice Bucke / London,
Ontario, Canada / Purchased at Public Sale in
London, England, by / The Ulysses Book shop,
Ltd. / Or by Private Treaty by / Dr. Jacob
Schwartz / London, England / To be Dispersed at
Public Sale / April 15 and 16, at 8:15 p.m. / [three
lines] / Foreword By Christopher Morley /
American Art Association / Anderson Galleries ·
Inc / 30 East 57th Street · New York / 1936
La. 8vo.
    Morley's foreword, entitled "Strong Sensual
    Germs," appears on pages [v]-[ix].

                    1937

The Adventures of / Hajji / Baba of Ispahan / by
James Morier / Illustrated by Cyrus Le Roy

Baldridge / [publisher's device] / Random House
inc. — New York / MCMXXXVII 4to. 406 pp.
Foreword by Christopher Morley appears on
pages [ix-xii] and is dated September, 1937.

Breaking into print / Being A Compilation Of
Papers / Wherein / Each Of A Select Group Of
Authors / Tells / Of The Difficulties Of Author-
ship / & / How Such Trials Are Met / Together
With / Biographical Notes And Comment / By An
Editor Of The Colophon / Elmer Adler / Now /
Put In A Book By Simon And Schuster / Publishers
Of New York In MCMXXXVII La. 8vo. 198 pp.
Christopher Morley's contribution "The Eighth
Sin" appears on pages 151-159. This contribu-
tion first appeared in Part Three of the
"Colophon," September, 1930. It is prefaced
in Adler's book by a brief biographical sketch
and two letters from Morley to the Editor, dated
January 28, 1937, and February 1, 1937.

[rule] / Essays / Then And Now / By / Alice
Cecilia Cooper / San Francisco Junior College /
Formerly Of University High School / Oakland,
California / and / David Fallon / [publisher's
device] / Ginn And Company / Boston · New York ·
Chicago · London · Atlanta · Dallas · Columbus ·
San Francisco / [rule] 12mo. 402 pp.
This volume contains a brief biographical sketch
of Morley and his essay "On Unanswering
Letters," pages 50-54; reprinted from "Mince
Pie" (1919).

The / (Old) / Farmer's Almanack, / Calculated
On A New And Improved Plan / For The Year Of
Our Lord / 1937 / [eight lines] / By Robert B.
Thomas. / [sketch] / [six lines] / [rule] / Copy-
right, 1936, By / Mabel M. Swan, / Brookline,
Mass. / [one line] 12mo. 108 pp.
Morley's "Ballade Of A Horoscope" appears

on page 48; reprinted from the "Saturday Review of Literature," January 18, 1936.

Recognition of / Robert Frost / [rule] / Twenty-Fifth Anniversary / Edited by / Richard Thornton / [ornament] / New York / Henry Holt and Company La. 8vo. 312 pp.
Morley contributes "Winesap Humor" which appears on pages 258-260. This is the first book printing of the essay, which appeared in the May 1936 issue of the "Book-of-the-Month Club News" as a review of Frost's book, "A Further Range."

A Savoyard / Chaplet / Issued, with original contributions by Christopher / Morley, Isaac Goldberg, Odell Shepard, William / Danforth, William Lyon Phelps, Carroll A. Wilson / and others, on the occasion of an exhibit of Gilbert / and Sullivan material from Mr. Wilson's collection / at the Olin Memorial Library, Wesleyan University / April 25th to June 20th, 1937 / [ornament] / Middletown, Conn. / Wesleyan University Library / 1937 8vo. 44 pp.
Morley's contribution "Gilbert And Sullivan," sub-titled "Their Foe Was Folly, and Their Weapon Wit" appears on page 21, signed Christopher Morley. / April 6, 1937. On page 20, opposite, is a facsimile of the manuscript copy of Morley's contribution with the additional note in the upper right hand corner, not in the printed copy, For the Wesleyan / G & S Festival. Though published as a separate, "A Savoyard Chaplet" is volume 7, no. 4, May 1937 of "About Books," Olin Library, Wesleyan University, Middletown, Conn. One thousand copies of this special issue of "About Books" were printed.

[Number 25] / Two Centuries Of / Bruce Rogers / With A Prologue / "BR's Secret Passion" / By /

Christopher Morley / [ornament] Philip C.
Duschnes / 507 Fifth Avenue, New York   12mo.
44 pp., Yellow wrappers.
  Five hundred and fifty copies of this catalogue
  were printed, February 1937 by D. B. Updike,
  The Merrymount Press, Boston. Morley's
  "BR's Secret Passion" appears on pages iii-
  [v]. First written for the Typophile's
  "Barnacles From Many Bottoms" (q.v.), it
  appeared as a separate in 1935 (Lee, page 116)
  and was reprinted in "BR Marks And Remarks"
  in 1946 (q.v.). An edition of "Two Centuries of
  Bruce Rogers," limited to fifty copies, was
  issued in bound, marbled boards, signed by both
  Morley and Rogers.

1938

Anthology Of / Magazine Verse / for 1937 / And
Yearbook Of / American Poetry / Edited by /
Alan F. Pater / New York / The Paebar Company,
Inc. / MCMXXXVIII   8vo. 227 pp.
  "To Hilaire Belloc" appears on page 113; re-
  printed from the "Commonweal," May 7, 1937.

The Book Detektive. Planned by Beach Cooke.
With an Admonition by Christopher Morley.
William Morrow & Co., New York, N. Y.
12 mo. Contents consist of a pamphlet, bookmarks, and printed cards enclosed in pockets on
the inside of a portfolio which folds into the shape
of a book.
  The bookmarks reprint Morley's "On The Return Of A Book Lent To A Friend," from "The
  Haunted Bookshop" (1919). The eight-page
  pamphlet reads Private / The / Book / Detektive's / Little Black Book / A Record / of
  the book-borrowing / habits of your friends /
  and / a most important / admonition by / Christopher Morley / being the hitherto / unpublished

transcript / of the Criminal Trial / Pandowdy
V. Librovore / [copyright note] / William
Morrow & Co. / 386 Fourth Ave., New York,
N. Y. Morley's admonition appears on pages
4-8 of the pamphlet.

A / Book of Poems / Selected And Edited / By /
Oliphant Gibbons / [two lines] / [ornament] / New
York Cincinnati Chicago / American Book
Company / Boston Atlanta Dallas San Francisco
12mo. 256 pp.
The poem "Smells" appears on pages 95-96;
reprinted from "Chimneysmoke" (1921).

Two / Songs / by / John Mundy / The Secret /
Price 50 cents / His Brown-Eyed / Mistress /
Price 50 cents / Poems by / Christopher / Mor-
ley / Sprague [publisher's device] Coleman / New
York Folio. 6 pp.
This composition includes only "His Brown-
Eyed Mistress." The words to the song were
contributed by Morley.

Kidnapped / Being Memoirs Of / The Adventures
of David Balfour / In The Year 1751: / How he
was Kidnapped and Cast away; his Sufferings in
a / Desert Isle; his Journey in the Wild Highlands;
his Acquain- / tance with Alan Breck Stewart and
other notorious Highland / Jacobites; with all that
he suffered at the hands of his Uncle, / Ebenezer
Balfour of Shaws, falsely so-called: / Written by
Himself, and now set forth, by / Robert Louis
Stevenson / [sketch] / Illustrated with wood engravings by Hans Alexander Mueller / And with
an Introduction by Christopher Morley / New
York · mcm xxx viii / For the Members of The
Limited Editions Club by the Pynson Printers
La. 8vo. 238 pp.
The introduction by Christopher Morley appears
on pages vii-[x]. There were 1500 copies of

this edition, all signed in autograph by the artist on page [238].

[ornament] The Typophiles [ornament] / Left to Their Own / Devices / [drawing] / 1937
16mo. 330 pp. Fancy wove paper. Blue linen, gold lettering. In slipcase.
  Page [v] carries a three-stanza poem by Christopher Morley entitled "A Salute to / Typophiles Desipient." The subscript is dated January, 1938. The copyright also is dated 1938, indicating that the title page was made sometime during the previous year.

[double rule] / Poems / for Modern Youth / [rule] / Edited By Adolph Gillis / [three lines] / And / William Rose Benét / [publisher's device] / Houghton Mifflin Company / Boston · New York · Chicago · Dallas · Atlanta · San Francisco / The Riverside Press Cambridge   12mo. 532 pp.
  Reprints "At The Mermaid Cafeteria" page [lx], "To A Post-Office Inkwell" page 120, "Of A Child That Had Fever" pages 149-150, "Smells" pages 150-151, "Reading Aloud" page 384, and "On A Portrait Of Dr. Samuel Johnson, LL.D." page 435.

Two / Songs / by / John Mundy / The Secret / Price 50 cents / The Brown-Eyed Mistress / Price 50 cents / Poems by / Christopher / Morley / Sprague [publisher's device] Coleman / New York   Folio. 6 pp.
  This composition includes only "The Secret." The words to the song were contributed by Morley.

A Cookbook / The Stag At Ease / Compiled by / Marian Squire / Being The Culinary Preferences / Of A Number Of Distinguished / Male Citizens Of The World / [double rule] / [publisher's de-

vice] / The Caxton Printers, Ltd. / Caldwell,
Idaho / 1938   8vo. 164 pp.
Morley contributes a recipe on pages 100-101.
He says his "favorite breakfast is fried apples
with Philadelphia scrapple and toasted corn
pone."

Walt Whitman / in Camden / A Selection of Prose
from Specimen Days / With a Preface by Chris-
topher Morley / and Photographs by Arnold
Genthe / Camden: The Haddon Craftsmen / 1938
Title page has ornamental border. 4to. 48 pp.
Laid paper, watermarked. Coarse line binding.
Boxed.
The preface by Christopher Morley appears on
pages [ix]-[xv]. Limited to 1100 copies.

1939

A Book Of / Children's Literature / Selected and
Edited / by / Lillian Hollowell / [three lines] /
[ornament] / [rule] / Farrar & Rinehart, Inc. ·
New York   La. 8vo. 942 pp.
"Animal Crackers" appears on pages 780-781;
reprinted from "Songs For A Little House"
(1917); "Smells (Junior)" on page 800 reprinted
from "The Rocking Horse" (1919).

The Bookman's / Guide to New York / [cut of New
York Public Library lions] / Photo by Ewing
Galloway, N. Y. / [monogram of Philip C.
Duschnes] / Philip C. Duschnes / 507 Fifth
Avenue, New York / MUrray Hill 2-2879   8vo.
32 pp.
Morley's contribution appears on the recto and
verso of the back cover and is a reprint from
"New York, One Way." This booklet was issued
in May, 1939, by a number of New York book-
shops, each carrying its own imprint on the
front cover and advertising matter on the inside

and outside back covers. Philip C. Duschnes used the third and fourth covers to reprint "New York, One Way," which appeared with changes under that title in the "Saturday Review of Literature," June 26, 1937. Prior to the "Saturday Review of Literature" printing, the full essay, under the title "Principality and Power" appeared in "New York World's Fair 1939" (q.v.).

[star] / Cordially / Yours . . . / [rule] / A Collection of Original Short Stories / and Essays by / America's Leading Authors / The Boston Herald / Book Fair Committee / [rule] / 1939   12mo. 96 pp.
Morley's contribution, entitled "History Of The Future," appears on pages 28-29. Thomas Page Smith is listed as editor of the volume on page 96. There were 10,000 copies of this book printed on October 19, of which 1495 copies were given imprint J. B. Lippincott Company / New York · Philadelphia · London · Toronto / [rule] / 1939

Goudy Gaudeamus / In celebration of the dinner / given Frederic W. Goudy / on his 74th birthday / March eighth / 1939 / Printed for the Distaff Side: 1939
16mo.   206 unnumbered pages, including tip-ins and blanks. Various papers. Bound in gray linen, front and back covered with fancy blue paper. Limited to 195 copies.
The Morley signature, entitled "Goudiamus Igitur," was also issued as a separate (q.v.).

[rule] / 1939 / Essay Annual / A Yearly Collection Of Significant Essays / Personal, Critical, Controversial, And / Humorous / [rule] / Erich A. Walter / Department Of English / University Of Michigan / [rule] / Scott, Foresman and Com-

pany / Chicago   Atlanta   Dallas   New York /
[rule] La. 8vo. 310 pp.
The Morley contribution, entitled "Mind Raid
Precautions," appears on pages 210-216. It
had its first printing in the "Saturday Review
of Literature," March 4, 1939.

Poems Of Today / A Collection Of The Contem-
porary / Verse Of America And Great Britain /
[double rule] / Edited by / Alice Cecilia Cooper /
[three lines] / Illustrated By Florence L. Heyn /
New Enlarged Edition / Ginn And Company /
Boston · New York · Chicago · London · Atlanta ·
Dallas · Columbus · San Francisco / [rule] 12mo.
412 pp.
"A Charm" appears on page 58; reprinted from
"Songs For A Little House" (1917). "Smells"
appears on pages 241-242; reprinted from
"The Rocking Horse" (1919).

The Seaman's / Library Manual / Prepared by
Herbert L. Howe / Librarian / [cut of a ship] /
New York / The American Merchant Marine /
Library Association / 1939 18mo. Twelve un-
numbered pages.
Morley's preface appears on the verso of the
title page.

Don Marquis / [sketch] / Sons Of / The Puritans /
With a Preface by Christopher Morley / Doubleday, Doran & Co., Inc., New York, 1939 8vo.
313 pp.
The Morley introduction appears on pages v-
viii. The jacket flaps also carry most of the
introduction.

1940

Baker Street and Beyond / A Sherlockian Gazet-
teer / Edgar W. Smith / with five detailed and
illustrated maps / from the pen of Julian

Wolff, M.D. / "I hear of Sherlock / every-
where . . . ." / —The Greek Interpreter   La.
8vo. 54 pp.
First edition 300 copies of which the first hundred were bound in de luxe binding. Morley's
contribution is the "Foreword" page 7, signed
Christopher Morley. / May 17, 1940.

Books Alive / By Vincent Starrett / [double rule] /
A Profane Chronicle / Of Literary Endeavor And /
Literary Misdemeanor / [rule] / With An Informal
Index By / Christopher Morley / [double rule] /
Random House. 1940. New York   La. 8vo.
360 pp.
Morley's index appears on eight unnumbered
pages preceding the Foreword, page 7. The
remarks preceding the index proper read
[double rule] / Signposts To What Is In This
Book / An Unconventional Index / By Christopher Morley / [double rule] / This is not an
index of names and topics, but rather an /
appetitive catalogue of ideas and undertones.
The amateur / indexer has even ventured occasionally to take issue with / the author;
correspondence, however, should be addressed /
solely to V.S., in care of the Publishers, en-
closing a stamped / envelope. / C. M. Pages
305-308 carry a long quote which is an original
contribution by Christopher Morley.

[row of ornaments] / Essays / For Discussion /
Revised Edition / Edited by / Anita P. Forbes,
A.M. / [publisher's device] / [rule] / Harper &
Brothers Publishers / New York And London
12mo. 560 pp.
"Ingo" appears on pages 257-261; reprinted
from "Shandygaff" (1918).

Kitty Foyliana / or / The Natural History of a
Natural / Being the special advertising campaign

112

reprinted from / the New York Times, in which
it appeared twice a / week during Kitty Foyle's
first Hundred Thousand / K F / J. B. Lippincott
Company / Philadelphia / 1940
12mo. 27 pp. Wove paper. French fold brown
wrappers.
   The publishers state that the text selections and
page arrangements were made by Christopher
Morley. Issued January 24, 1940, with a first
printing of 1500 copies.

[green leaf border design vertically on page from
top to bottom] / Walt Whitman / Leaves / Of /
Grass / Selected And With / An Introduction /
By Christopher Morley / Illustrations / By Lewis
C. Daniel / Doubleday, Doran & Co., Inc. / New
York: MC MXL   4to. 316 pp.
   In addition to selecting the poetry and prose
contained in this edition, Morley wrote "An
Introduction to the Leaves" which appears on
pages v-xiii.

Story and Verse / for Children / [eagle] / [rule] /
Selected and Edited by / Miriam Blanton Huber,
Ph.D. / Decorations by Boris Artzybasheff / The
Macmillan Company / New York MCMXL   La.
8vo. 857 pp.
   The poem "Song For A Little House" appears
on page 164; reprinted from "Chimneysmoke"
(1921).

A Treasury Of / The World's / Great Letters /
From Ancient Days To Our Own Time / containing
The Characteristic And Crucial Communications, /
And Intimate Exchanges And Cycles Of Corre-
spondence, Of / Many Of The Outstanding Figures
Of World History, And Some / Notable Contem-
poraries, Selected, Edited, And Integrated / With
Biographical Backgrounds And Historical
Settings / And Consequences By M. Lincoln

Schuster / [publisher's device] / New York
Simon And Schuster MCMXXXX   La. 8vo.
563 pp.
   Christopher Morley's letter to T. A. Daly
   appears on pages 500-505 under the heading
   "Christopher Morley Inspires The Tale Of A
   WAYSIDE INN."

A Tribute To / A. Edward Newton / Christmas /
1940 / The Library Of / Congress
12mo. 28 unnumbered pages. Wove paper. Heavy
blue paper covers. Stitched with silk cord.
   Morley's contribution appears on pages [7-8],
   signed Christopher Morley. Issued from the
   Rare Book Room of the Library of Congress
   in an edition of one thousand copies, December,
   1940, and published by the United States Gov-
   ernment Printing Office. A second issue appeared January, 1941.

221B [in rule box] / Studies in Sherlock Holmes /
By / Various Hands / Edited by Vincent Starrett /
[rule] / New York The Macmillan Company /
1940 8vo. 248 pp.
   Morley contributes the essay "Was Sherlock
   Holmes An American?" which appears on
   pages 5-15 and first appeared in the "Saturday
   Review of Literature," July 21, 1934. Morley
   contributed the introductory paragraph to the
   letter by F. V. Morley entitled "A Sherlock
   Holmes Cross-word" appearing on pages 244-
   247. This was reprinted with some changes
   from the "Saturday Review of Literature" May
   19, 1934, and also appeared as a separate
   (q.v.).

1941

AYH / Handbook / 1941 / AYH Inc., Northfield,
Mass. 16mo. 128 pp.

Morley contributes an introduction entitled
"And A Sun-Burned Nose" to the American
Youth Hostels, Inc. handbook, pages 29-32.

Poems / for a Machine Age / [rule] / Selected
and Edited by / Horace J. McNeil / [two lines] /
with the editorial collaboration of Clarence
Stratton / [two lines] / [rule] / McGraw-Hill Book
Company, Inc. / New York and London   8vo.
568 pp.
"Mandarin On The Air" from "Streamlines"
(1936) appears on pages 32-33. "Smells" from
"The Rocking Horse" (1919) appears on page
214. "In Honor Of Taffy Topaz" from
"Chimneysmoke" (1921) appears on page 403.
"To A Very Young Gentleman" from "The
Rocking Horse" (1919) appears on page 440.

The / Readers Digest / Reader / Selected By /
Theodore Roosevelt / And The Staff Of The /
Reader's Digest / [publisher's device] / [rule] /
Doubleday, Doran & Company, Inc. / New York
1941 8vo. 495 pp.
Morley's essay "The World's Most Famous
Oration" appears on page 222; reprinted from
"Pipefuls" (1920).

1942

Innocent / Merriment / An Anthology of Light
Verse / Selected By / Franklin P. Adams /
("F.P.A.") / Whittlesey House / McGraw-Hill
Book Company, Inc. / New York · London   La.
8vo. 523 pp.
"The Gospel of Mr. Pepys" appears on pages
158-159; "A Grub Street Recessional" pages
289-290.

Letters from Baker Street / A communication
appearing in the London Times of July 3, 1890,

from / an amateur reasoning of some celebrity; and a communication / appearing in the Daily Gazette in March or April, 1892, over / the signature of a well-known criminal investigator. / Together with the stories in which these letters are quoted: / The Lost Special / and / The Man With The Watches / by / Sir Arthur Conan Doyle / Illuminated by a noteworthy communication from Stanley Hopkins, O.B.E., / Chief Inspector C. I. D. (Retired), written and received / through the good offices of / Christopher Morley / and further illuminated by a communication from the eminent Holmesian scholar / Vincent Starrett / Edited and Examined for the Canons / by / Edgar W. Smith / "You can file it in our archives, Watson." / — The Adventure Of The Retired Colourman   La. 8vo. 60 pp.

400 copies printed of which 200 were bound in de luxe binding. Morley's "A Letter From Roslyn Heights, New York" appears on page 15 and is signed in autograph facsimile Green Escape / Roslyn Heights, / New York. / April 15, 1942.

New Directions / Number Seven / 1942 / [publisher's device] / Published by New Directions / Norfolk · Connecticut
La. 8vo. 494 pp. (6 additional unnumbered).
The Morley contribution, a brief tribute to Ford Madox Ford, appears on pages 476-477.

The Pocket / Companion / Edited and with an introduction by / Philip Van Doren Stern / Pocket Books Inc. [publisher's device] New York, 20, N. Y. 16mo. 493 pp.
"Smells" appears on page 442; reprinted from "Chimneysmoke" (1921).

America's 93 Greatest Living Authors Present / This Is My Best / [ornament] Over 150 Self-

Chosen And / Complete Masterpieces, Together
With / Their Reasons For Their Selections /
[publisher's device] Edited by Whit Burnett /
Burton C. Hoffman The Dial Press New York,
1942   8vo. 1180 pp.
  Morley's contribution, consisting of four poems
  and a note explaining what and why he contributed to the anthology, appears on pages 618-
  621. "Nightpiece To Herrick" makes its first
  appearance in print here. "Hampstead Coach"
  was reprinted from "Stack" (Haverford College)
  Autumn, 1940. "A Song For Eros" is reprinted
  from "The Trojan Horse," and "Dogwood
  Tree" from "Saturday Review of Literature,"
  June 28, 1930. A brief biography and list of
  works by Morley appear on page 1148.

1943

Choice Poems / for / Elementary Grades / Compiled By / Matilda Mahaffey Elsea / B.S., M.A. /
[publisher's device] / Published By / The Edwards
Press / "The Hillbilly Printers" / Osceola, Mo.
8vo. 230 pp.
  Reprints "Animal Crackers" page 16, "The
  Milkman" page 46, "Song For A Little House"
  page 89, and "The Engineer" pages 98-99.

Tom Sawyer / And / Huckleberry Finn / [orna-
ment] / [Mark Twain] / London: J. M. Dent & Sons
Ltd. / New York: E. P. Dutton & Co. Inc.   16mo.
435 pp.
  Morley contributes the "Introduction" pages
  vii-xi.

Under / The Tent Of / The Sky / A Collection of
Poems About / Animals Large And Small / Se-
lected by / John E. Brewton / [sketch] / . . . with /
Drawings by / Robert / Lawson / The Macmillan
Company / New York / MCMXLIII   La. 8vo.

205 pp.
"Animal Crackers" appears on pages 23-24, reprinted from "Songs For A Little House" (1917); also "The Moon-Sheep" on page 140 from the same.

1944

A Baker Street Four-Wheeler / Sixteen Pieces Of / Sherlockiana / Edited by / Edgar W. Smith / [four lines] La. 8vo. 77 pp.
Morley's "Sherlock Holmes's Prayer" appears on pages 16-17.

The Essayes / Or Counsels Civill & Morall / Of / Francis Bacon / Baron Of Verulam / Viscount Saint Alban / New York / The Limited Editions Club / 1944 Folio. 190 pp.
1100 copies printed for members of the Club by the Press of William E. Rudge's Sons under the direction of Bruce Rogers. The introduction by Christopher Morley appears on pages [v]-viii.

Essays Of / Yesterday And Today / Edited by John A. Lester / Hill School, Pottstown, Pennsylvania / Illustrated by Susanne Suba / [sketch] / Harcourt, Brace And Company / New York 1944 Chicago 12mo. 376 pp.
"On Unanswering Letters" appears on pages [179]-182; reprinted from "Essays" (1928).

Literary / England / Photographs Of Places / Made Memorable / In English Literature / By David E. Scherman & Richard Wilcox / A Preface by Christopher Morley / [photograph] / Published by Random House New York 4to. Paging unnumbered.
Morley's introduction, entitled "A Preface: The Sense of Place" appears on pages [5-10].

Profile / By / Gaslight / An Irregular Reader /
About the Private Life of / Sherlock Holmes /
Edited By / Edgar W. Smith / 1944 / Simon And
Schuster / New York   8vo. 312 pp.
  Morley's contribution "Clinical Notes By A
  Resident Patient" appears on pages 48-59.

Sherlock Holmes / And Dr. Watson / A Textbook
of Friendship / Edited By / Christopher Morley /
[publisher's device] / Harcourt, Brace and Company / New York   12mo. 366 pp.
  Morley's contributions are extensive. His "Introduction" appears on pages [1]-22 preceded
  by a one page preface "Memorandum" which
  appears on page [iii] and is signed C. M. / New
  York City, November, 1943. The five Sherlock
  Holmes stories reprinted in the volume are
  annotated by Morley. Each story is followed by
  "Topics for Discussion," intended by Morley
  for younger readers. An annotated list of the
  Holmes stories, entitled "A Guide to the Complete Sherlock Holmes" and chronologically
  arranged by date of publication in book form,
  appears on pages [351]-364. A select bibliography of Sherlockiana entitled "Notes for Ad-
  vanced Students" appears on pages 365-366.
  The back of the book jacket has an original piece
  by Christopher Morley on behalf of the Fourth
  War Loan. It is entitled The Adventure of the
  F.W.L. / Being a reprint from the Reminiscences / of John H. Watson, M.D. A specially
  printed leaflet entitled "Sherlock Holmes's
  Prayer" was brought out in connection with
  this book by the publisher (q.v.).

1945

A Garland for / Goudy / Being Verses, Old and
New, / Gathered for his Eightieth Birthday /
March Eighth · 1945 / [decorative "80" (made

up of Goudy ornaments by Paul McPharlin)] /
Privately Printed by His Friends 12mo. 38 pp.
Laid paper. Bound in cloth and boards: flowered
paper sides, natural linen backstrip with paper
label.
  "Goudiamus Igitur," by Christopher Morley,
appears on pp. 24-26, with the footnote, "This
poem was written for the Distaff Side dinner
on Goudy's 74th birthday." The colophon reads,
"Two hundred twenty copies of / "A Garland
for Goudy" / have been printed at the / Peter
Pauper Press / and bound at / The George
Grady Press / [leaf]. "Goudiamus Igitur"
appeared in the collection "Goudy Goudiamus"
(q.v.) and as a separate (q.v.).

Orchids To / Murder / by / Hulbert Footner /
[publisher's device] / Publishers / Harper &
Brothers / New York · London   12mo. 244 pp.
  The introduction by Morley, entitled "Hulbert
Footner (1877-1944)" appears on pages v-x.

Poet To Poet / A Treasury of Golden Criticism /
Edited by Houston Peterson / and William S.
Lynch / New York / Prentice-Hall, Inc. 1945
8vo. 368 pp.
  A poem about Austin Dobson by Morley appears
on pages 320-321. Reprinted from "Parson's
Pleasure" (1923).

1946

The Best of / Don Marquis / with an introduction
by / Christopher Morley / and with illustrations
by / George Harriman / [publisher's device] /
Garden City, New York 1946 / Doubleday & Company, Inc. 12mo. 670 pp.
  Morley's introduction appears on pages xiii-
xxx. It was first delivered as The Annual
Hopwood Address, June 2, 1937, at the Univer-

sity of Michigan, and appeared initially in print
under the title "A Successor To Mark Twain"
in the "Michigan Alumnus Quarterly Review,"
Summer, 1937.

B R Marks / & Remarks / [ornamental rule] /
The marks by Bruce Rogers, et al. / The re-
marks by his friends: H. W. Kent, / J. M. Bowles,
Carl Purlington Rollins, / David Pottinger, Chris-
topher Morley, / James Hendrickson & Frederic
Warde / [ornament] The whole gathered and pub-
lished / by The Typophiles in New York, 1946.
12mo. 149 pp.
   Published in a limited edition of 400 copies.
Contains Morley's essay on Bruce Rogers
"B.R.'s Secret Passion," pages 123-127.
Written first for The Typophile's "Barnacles
From Many Bottoms" (q.v.), it appeared as a
separate in 1935 (Lee, page 116) and was also
reprinted in "[Number 25] Two Centuries Of
Bruce Rogers" (q.v.).

Great / Teachers / Portrayed By Those Who /
Studied Under Them / Edited with an Introduction
by / Houston Peterson / [publisher's device] /
New Brunswick / Rutgers University Press /
MCMXLVI 8vo. 351 pp.
   The Morley contribution "Quaker Scholar"
appears on pages 123-128, a reprint of "In
Memoriam: Francis Barton Gummere" which
appeared in "Plum Pudding" (1921).

Journeys / In Time / From The Halls Of Monte-
zuma / To Patagonia's Plains / A treasury,
garnered from four centuries / of writers (1519-
1942), with comments, / profiles, and personal
experiences / By Blair Niles / [double rule] /
Coward-McCann, Inc., New York 8vo. 404 pp.
   A selection from "Hasta La Vista" appears on
pages 281-284. It is preceded by a note about

the book by the compiler, entitled "Christopher Morley's Postcard" pages 280-281.

Murder / with a difference / Three Unusual Crime Novels / Selected And With An Introduction / By Christopher Morley / Random House. New York 8vo. 563 pp.
Morley's "Introduction" occupies pages vii-x, and is signed in autograph facsimile Christopher Morley / Roslyn Heights, N. Y. / June 18, 1946. Parts of the introduction on the back of the jacket and the front flap.

Strange And / Fantastic Stories / [rule] / Fifty Tales of Terror, / Horror And Fantasy / [rule] Edited by Joseph A. Margolies / Introduction by / Christopher Morley / Whittlesey House / McGraw-Hill Book Company, Inc. / New York: London 8vo. 762 pp.
The Morley introduction appears on pages vii-x.

To / Doctor R. / [ornament] / Essays Here Collected and / Published in Honor of the / Seventieth Birthday / of / Dr. A. S. W. Rosenbach / July 22, 1946 / Philadelphia 1946   La. 8vo. 301 pp.
Morley's essay "The Atom Splitter" appears on pages [174]-179.

The / Treasure Chest / An Anthology / Of Contemplative Prose / Edited by J. Donald Adams / [publisher's device] / New York: / E. P. Dutton & Company, Inc. / 1946   12mo. 402 pp.
Brief excerpts from "Human Being" and "John Mistletoe" appear on pages 330-331.

1947

"Jive's like that" / Being The Life And Times Of / Our / Bill / by Haenigsen / With A Preface By / Christopher Morley / The Procyon Press

Inc. / New York   4to. 96 unnumbered pages.
The Morley preface appears on pages [5-6] and
is signed Christopher Morley / Roslyn Heights,
L. I. / November, 1946

The / Life & Opinions / Of / Tristam Shandy /
Gentleman / [two lines] / By / Lawrence Sterne /
[rule] With an Introduction by Christopher Morley / and Illustrations by / T. M. Cleland / [rule] /
New York / The Heritage Press   4to. 444 pp.
The Morley "Introduction" appears on pages
[v]-viii.

1948

American Essays / Edited, with an introduction
and notes / By Charles B. Shaw / [publisher's
device] / A Pelican Mentor Book / Published By
The New American Library / [publisher's device]
12mo. 180 pp.
Morley's contribution, entitled "Three Kinds
Of Collectors," appears on pages 149-163. It
appeared first as Chapter II of "Ex Libris
Carissimis" (1932). The editor contributes a
brief biographical sketch of Morley on page 149.

Anthology of / Children's Literature / [illustration
in color] / Compiled By Edna Johnson, Carrie E. /
Scott & Evelyn R. Sickels. Illustra- / tions In Full
Color By N. C. Wyeth / Houghton · Mifflin · Com-
pany · Boston / The Riverside Press Cambridge
La. 8vo. 1114 pp.
Contains "Animal Crackers" page 884, re-
printed from "Songs For A Little House" (1917);
"Smells," page 884, reprinted from "Poems"
(1919); "The Plumpuppets" page 885, reprinted
from "Poems" (1919); and "Song For A Little
House" page 885, reprinted from "The Rocking
Horse" (1919).

The Best / Short Short Stories / From Collier's /
Selected, With An Introduction And Notes, By /
Barthold Fles / [publisher's device] / Cleveland
And New York / The World Publishing Company
8vo. 256 pp.
Morley's story "A Good Deed" appears on
pages 71-74 and is a reprint from "Collier's",
August 23, 1930.

Tribute To / Walter De La Mare / on his /
Seventy-fifth birthday   8vo. 196 pp.
Printed in a very small edition by Faber and
Faber Limited, 24 Russell Square, London, few
if any copies reached this country. Morley's
contribution bears no title but appears on pages
192-193. The "Tribute" has a colored litho-
graph frontispiece by Barnet Freedman, two
half-tones, one reproduction of a portrait drawing by William Rothenstein, a caricature by
Max Beerbohm, and a facsimile manuscript
page.

The Adventures Of Sherlock Holmes / The Ad-
venture Of / The Blue Carbuncle / By A. Conan
Doyle / [ornament] / With An Introduction By
Christopher Morley / Edited and with a Biblio-
graphical Note by Edgar W. Smith / The Baker
Street Irregulars, Inc., Publishers / New York ~
1948   La. 8vo. 64 pp.
Morley contributes the introduction entitled
"The Blue Carbuncle or, The Season of For-
giveness" pages 9-16, signed Christopher
Morley / Green Escape, Roslyn, N. Y. /
Christmas, 1948.

The Adventures Of Sherlock Holmes / The Adventure Of / The Blue Carbuncle / By A. Conan
Doyle / [ornament] / With An Introduction By
Christopher Morley / Edited and with a Bibliographical Note by Edgar W. Smith / The Baker

Street Irregulars, Inc., Publishers / New York~
1948   La. 8vo.   76 pp.
The Morley introduction in this Deluxe edition
is the same as in the trade edition. This edition
has added "A Note On The Baker Street Irregulars" pages 67-75 which is taken largely
from Morley's column "Clinical Notes By A
Resident Patient" appearing in the "Baker
Street Journal."

The / Pleasures / of Smoking / as expressed by /
Those Poets, Wits / and / Tellers of Tales / who
have drawn their inspiration from / The Fragrant
Weed / · / compiled by Sylvestre C. Watkins / · /
Henry Schuman / New York   La. 8vo.   203 pp.
"My Pipe" from "Poems" (1929) appears on
pages 16-17; "Another Letter to Lord C__ __"
from the "Saturday Review of Literature"
February 10, 1945 appears on pages 123-124;
"The Last Pipe" from "Shandygaff" (1918)
appears on pages 140-144.

The Pleasures / of Walking / [rule] / [ornament] /
Edited By / Edwin Valentine Mitchell / Author of
"It's an Old New England Custom," / "It's an
Old Pennsylvania Custom," "Yankee Folk," etc. /
[rule] / New York · The Vanguard Press, Inc.
8vo.   172 pp.
Morley's essay "Sauntering" from "Travels in
Philadelphia" (1920) appears on pages 118-122.

[ornamental rule] / Red Wine of Youth / A Life
of Rupert Brooke / [single rule] / By Arthur
Stringer / Illustrated / [single rule] / The Bobbs-
Merrill Company / Publishers / Indianapolis /
New York   8vo.   287 pp.
Morley's poem "To Rupert Brooke," reprinted
from "Chimneysmoke" (1921), appears on
pages [9-12].

Noble's Comparative Classics / [rule] / Comparative Essays / Present And Past / Revised and Enlarged / Edited by / Warren W. Read / [4 lines of type] / [publisher's device] / Noble and Noble, Publishers, Inc. / 67 Irving Place New York 3, N. Y. 12mo. 477 pp.
"On unanswering letters" appears on pp. 352-57.

1949

World's Greatest / Christmas Stories / Edited by / Eric Posselt / Ziff-Davis Publishing Company / Chicago · New York 8vo. 451 pp.
"The Tree That Didn't Get Trimmed" appears on pages 31-36.

1950

Boswell's / London Journal / 1762-1763 / Now First Published From The Original Manuscript / Prepared For The Press, With Introduction And Notes / By Frederick A. Pottle / Sterling Professor Of English, Yale University / With A Preface By Christopher Morley / [publisher's device] / McGraw-Hill Book Company, Inc. / New York London Toronto
La. 8vo. 370 pp.
The preface appears on pages ix-xxix and first appeared in abbreviated form in the "Saturday Review of Literature" October 7, 1950.

The Challenge / of Ideas / An Essay Reader / Edited by / John Gehlmann / Oak Park & River Forest High School / Oak Park, Illinois / [publisher's device] / The Odeyssey Press . . . New York 8vo. 432 pp.
The essay "Ingo," from "Shandygaff" (1918), appears on pages 17-22.

The / Human Side / Of Bookplates / [publisher's
device] / The Ward Ritchie Press / 1951   8vo.
158 pp.
   Chapter 18, pages 125-133, contains portions
   of letters from Christopher Morley to the
   author Louise Seymour Jones.

A / Century of / Philadelphia Cricket / Edited by
John A. Lester / Philadelphia / University of
Pennsylvania Press / 1951
La. 8vo. 397 pp. with an appendix of 49 plates.
   Morley's "Footnote on Philadelphia Cricket,"
   dated Roslyn Heights, L.I., March 15, 1951,
   appears on pages xv-xviii.

IV. BOOKS CONTAINING MATERIAL ABOUT CHRISTOPHER MORLEY

Books containing material about Morley which are listed in the Lee bibliography are referred to here by title only, followed by a page reference to where the collation in Lee may be found and by the date of the title. Short collations are given for all biographical material omitted from Lee published since the Lee bibliography made its appearance.

OUR POETS OF TODAY (239)
    1918

CHRISTOPHER MORLEY, A BIOGRAPHICAL
   SKETCH (239)
    1922

OUR AMERICAN HUMORISTS (240)
    1922

AMERICAN NIGHTS ENTERTAINMENT (240)
    1923

THE MEN WHO MAKE OUR NOVELS (241)
    1924

MILDRED PALMER CAIN'S COPY OF CHRISTO-
   PHER MORLEY'S "PARNASSUS ON WHEELS"
   (241-242)
    1925

CHRISTOPHER MORLEY, MULTI EX UNO (242)
    1927

SIXTEEN AUTHORS TO ONE (242-243)
    1928

AMERICAN ESTIMATES (243)
    1929

AMERICAN FIRST EDITIONS (243-244)
    1929

BIRD'S-EYE VIEW OF HOBOKEN (244-245)
1929

CHRISTOPHER MORLEY—HIS BOOKS IN FIRST
EDITION (245)
1930

THE MYSTERY OF THE FOLDED PAPER
1930
The Mystery / of the / Folded Paper /~~~ by
~~~/ Hulbert Footner / Author of / "The
Doctor Who Held Hands" / "The Owl Taxi" /
[publisher's device] / Harper & Brothers—Publishers / New York and London / Established /
1817
12mo. Wove paper. 350 pp. Light green buckram.
There is some material about Morley in this
book. The scene of the novel is laid in Hoboken
and New York City, and the characters include
Christopher Morley, David Bone, Felix Reisen-
berg, and other members of the Three-Hours-
for-Lunch Club.

REVIEWING TEN YEARS (246)
1933

1935

A / Bibliography / Of / Christopher Morley / By /
Alfred P. Lee / [ornament] / "Check'd like a
bondman; all his faults observ'd, / Set in a note-
book, learn'd, and conn'd by rote." / Julius
Caesar, Act IV, Scene 3 / Doubleday, Doran &
Company, Inc. / Garden City / 1935 / New York
8vo. 277 pp.
The standard bibliography of Christopher Mor-

ley for separate writings published through
1934. It also includes short collations of the
books to which Morley contributed and of books
about Morley.

Creating / The Modern / American Novel / By
Harlan Hatcher / Farrar & Rinehart / Incorpo-
rated / On Murray Hill, New York   12mo.   307 pp.
The sketch on Christopher Morley appears on
pages 211-214 in the chapter entitled "Fantasy
As A Way Of Escape."

Living Authors / A Book of Biographies / Edited
by Dilly Tante / and Illustrated with 371 Photographs and Drawings / [ornament] / The H. W.
Wilson Company / New York / 1935   4to.   466 pp.
Biography and criticism appear on pages 281-
282; portrait on page 281.

1936

Catalogue 23 / "The Eighth Sin on Parnassus /
or / Where The Blues Begin." / First Editions,
Rare Trivia, & Pamphlets / of / Christopher
Morley / [double rule] / [publisher's device] /
[double rule] / Philip C. Duschnes / 507 Fifth
Avenue / New York, N. Y.
Priced catalogue of Morleyana issued November
1936, containing 65 "first editions, rare trivia
and pamphlets." This was the first printed
dealer's catalogue devoted entirely to Morley.

Portraits And / Self-Portraits / Collected And
Illustrated By / Georges Schreiber / 1936 /
Houghton Mifflin Company   Boston / The River-
side Press Cambridge   4to.   175 pp.
Morley's autobiographical sketch entitled
" 'Pocimur' ", appears on pages 111-115. It
is preceded by a four-line biographical note,

page 109, and portrait sketch of Morley by
Georges Schreiber.

1937

The Itinerary of Lippincott's Representative
William J. Finneran / On His Record Making,
23-Day, 22,000-Mile, Trip Around the United
States / for the purpose of Securing Prompt Distribution of Christopher Morley's New Novel /
"The Trojan Horse"   Broadside, yellow paper.
A schedule of the trip via the American Air
Lines, from October 17 to November 12. On
the reverse, a publisher's list of "Unforgettable
Books" by Christopher Morley. Accompanying
the broadside was a map, giving route and stop-
overs, with reading material same as that of
the Itinerary sheet. Buff calendared paper.
Issued September 28, 1937, 2000 copies. Map
issued October 7, 1937, 2700 copies.

Felix Riesenberg / Living Again / An Autobiography / [publisher's device] / MCMXXXVII /
Doubleday, Doran & Company, Inc. / Garden City
New York   8vo. 339 pp.
The main sketch of Morley appears on pages
321-336. Morley first suggested the book to
the author.

Portraits of / Thirty Authors / By Leonebel
Jacobs / Foreword by John Erskine / [author's
monogram, in brown] / Charles Scribner's Sons
New York / Charles Scribner's Sons Ltd   London / 1937   Folio. 10 preliminary pages.
The biographical notes, by Desmond Hall, are
on recto of protection leaves.

1940

[silhouette of Franklin] / Catalogue / No. Four /

of / The Franklin Bookshop / 107 South Twelfth
Street / Philadelphia, Pennsylvania / First Editions Of / Christopher Morley / The Definitive
Collection / Of Alfred P. Lee   12mo. 64 pp.
Lists 584 titles by and about Morley, including
a few magazine contributions. Contains an introduction by H. Tatnall Brown, Jr., dated
August 30, 1940. An earlier catalogue, entitled
Catalogue No. 2, undated, 28 pages, featuring
first editions of Christopher Morley, contained
85 Morley titles (15 pp.) including books,
pamphlets, and magazine contributions.

Contemporary / American Authors / A Critical
Survey and 219 Bio-Bibliographies / Fred B.
Millett / New York / Harcourt, Brace and Com-
pany / 1940   La. 8vo. 716 pp.
Critical comment on Morley on pages 160-161.
Biographical account, bibliography, studies and
articles about Morley appear on pages 497-503.

                    1942

Merle Johnson's / American First Editions /
Fourth Edition / [ornaments] / Revised And En-
larged By / Jacob Blanck / New York : R. R.
Bowker Co. 8vo. 553 pp.
A selective checklist of Morley first editions,
also secondary items, appears on pages 377-385.

Twentieth Century / Authors / A Biographical
Dictionary of Modern Literature / Edited by /
Stanley J. Kunitz / and / Howard Haycraft / Com-
plete In One Volume With / 1850 Biographies And /
1700 Portraits / [publisher's device] / New York /
The H. W. Wilson Company / Nineteen Hundred
Forty-Two   4to. 1578 pp.
The sketch of Morley, largely autobiographical,
appears on pages 986-988. Portions of this

sketch appeared first in the Chicago Daily News,
December 27, 1939.

1943

F. V. Morley / [rule] / My one Contribution to /
Chess / [publisher's device] / Le jeu vant la
chardelle / [rule] / New York · B. W. Huebsch ·
1945 12mo. 114 pp.
It contains considerable biographical information about the Morley family, frequent reference
to Christopher Morley, and several footnotes
by Christopher Morley. Another edition appeared in 1946 bearing the imprint George W.
Stewart, Publisher, Inc. / New York / 1946

1946

A History of / American Poetry / 1900-1940 /
Horace Gregory and / Marya Zaturenska / New
York / Harcourt, Brace And Company 8vo.
524 pp.
Brief critical comment appears on pages 306,
365, 444.

Writers and Writing / by Robert van Gelder /
Charles Scribner's Sons New York 1946 8vo.
381 pp.
The article on Morley occupies pages 334-338.
It is entitled "An Interview With Christopher
Morley."

1947

Books / and / Bipeds / By / Vincent Starrett /
[ornament] / Argus Books, Inc. / New York La.
8vo. 268 pp.
Notes on Morley appear on pages 27-28, 40-41,
106-107, 128, 130-135, and 199-200.

Who's Who / In America / [one line of type] / A
Biographical Dictionary Of Notable Living Men
And Women / Revised And Reissued Biennially /
Monthly Supplement / (Since 1939) / Vol. 26 /
1950-1951 / Two Years / Founded 1897 And Pub-
lished Since 1899 By / The A. N. Marquis Com-
pany / Chicago—11 U.S.A. / 1950   4to. 3347 pp.
  Brief biography of Morley appears on page 1949.
  Morley was first listed in "Who's Who in
  America" in the 1918-1919 edition.

Who's Who / 1951 / An / Annual Biographical
Dictionary / With Which Is Incorporated / "Men
and Women Of The Times" / One Hundred And
Third / Year Of Issue / London: Adam & Charles
Black / New York: The Macmillan Company
8vo. 3160 pp.
  Brief biographical sketch of Morley appears on
  page 2027. Morley's biographical sketch appeared for the first time in "Who's Who" in
  1944.

American Novelists / Of Today / [rule] / Harry
R. Warfel / American Book Company / New York
Cincinnati, Chicago   Boston   Atlanta   Dallas
San Francisco   La. 8vo. 478 pp.
  Excellent brief biographical sketch with some
  comment on individual works appears on pages
  308-310.

V. PERIODICAL ARTICLES BY
CHRISTOPHER MORLEY

No bibliography of Christopher Morley's periodical contributions will ever be complete. What follows is as accurate and complete as the compilers
could make it. Practically everything of importance
in periodical form has been reprinted by the author
in his collected writings. This is especially true of
the articles which Morley wrote as a columnist for
several newspapers and magazines and for this rea-
son the latter are omitted from the periodical listing
which follows. A word about these columns may
serve as a guide to future students and critics. As
columnist for the Philadelphia Evening Public
Ledger, Morley's daily stint appeared on the editorial page from 1918 to 1920. Among the numerous
headings used in the column are Travels in Philadelphia (most of these appeared later in book form
under the same title), The Chaffing Dish, The Electric Chair, and Prunes and Prisms. The column
was occasionally signed but more frequently appeared under the pseudonym Socrates. His favorite
topics in this column are food, books, and streets.
William McFee and Mrs. Etsu Inagaki Sugimoto were
introduced to readers in this country through the
Philadelphia column. In the early twenties Morley
contributed regularly to the New York Evening Post
under the gracious label The Bowling Green. Here
again he was instrumental in giving a wide audience
to many writers who have since become famous. In
the decade following the Post engagement Morley
supplied the Saturday Review of Literature with The
Bowling Green which contributed so much to that
magazine's brilliance. For a slightly shorter period
of time he contributed Trade Winds to the same
magazine under the pseudonym P.E.G. Quercus.
The Latin student will readily recognize the name
as an abbreviation for what in translation reads
"From little acorns oaks." A critical anthology of
Morley's writings would draw heavily on The Bowling Green, which included much of the long series
of light verse Translations from the Chinese, the

141

novel <u>Human</u> <u>Being</u>, and several of the collected editions of essays.

1908

The pine woods. Haverfordian 30:126, November

To a grasshopper. Haverfordian 30:162, December

1909

The limerick. Haverfordian 30:179-182, January; reprint, 51:76-82, January, 1932

To a skull. Haverfordian 30:168, January

Episodes in the life of an Irish waitress. Haverfordian 30:195-198, February; 31:7-10, March; 31:120-123, October

Skating song. Haverfordian 30:207, February. Same. American Childhood 12:55, January, 1927

To her. Haverfordian 31:1, March

A grand opera incident. Haverfordian 31:36-39, April

The letters of Robert Louis Stevenson. Haverfordian 31:57-63, May

Pirates. Haverfordian 31:65-71, May

The stargazer. Haverfordian 31:123, October

Omnia vincit amor. Haverfordian 31:163-168, December

1910

The claret of baccaral. Haverfordian 31:194-197, January

1913

Letter suggesting an epitaph for the Titanic and Vulturne. New York Times, November 28

Cedar chest. Outlook 105:802, December 13; Same. Literary Digest 55:61, December 8, 1917

1914

Kipling and the joy of life. Book News Monthly 32:274-275, February

"Chance": a great novel. Book News Monthly 32:384-385, April

What America thinks of war. World's Work 28:134, September (Signed C.D.M.)

1916

The superhawk. New York Times, July 16

Ballad of dandelion wine. Life 68:101, July 20

The wakeful husband. Independent 87:456, September 25

An apology for Boccaccio. Smart Set 50:257-263, November

Pedometer. Century 93:272, December

The man worth knowing. Life 68:1024, December 7

Question of plumage. Bellman 22:72-75, January 20

A charm for a new fireplace to stop its smoking. McClure's Magazine 48:62, February

Elegy written in a country coal bin. Century 93: 639-640, February

O. Henry—apothecary. Everybody's Magazine 36:166, February; Same. Current Opinion 62: 209, March

On first looking into a subway excavation. Century 93:796, March

Six weeks old. Collier's 58:11, March 3

The young mother. Collier's 59:13, March 31

The frantic astronomer. House and Garden 31:26, April

Peter Pan. Collier's 59:11, April 21

America, 1917. Collier's 59:23, April 28

Ten little cocktails. Collier's 59:34, May 19

The man. Ladies' Home Journal 34:14, June

Smells. Bookman 45:384, June; Same. Collier's 60:20, February 16, 1918

My pipe. Collier's 59:28, June 23

Madonna of the curb. Ladies' Home Journal 34:14, August

To a post office inkwell. Collier's 60:38, September 15; Same. Current Opinion 67:55, July, 1919; Same. Golden Book Magazine 10:93, December, 1929

To a discarded mirror. Ladies' Home Journal 34:16, October (The poem is printed so that it must be read through a mirror.)

The church of unbent knees. Collier's 60:30, October 6

To my wife. Collier's 60:23, October 27

Letter on the spirit at Camp Dix. New York Times, October 28

Inscription for a dog kennel. House and Garden 32:26, November

Reading aloud. Literary Digest 55:61, December 8

To the Oxford men in the war. Literary Digest 55:61-62, December 8

Rhubarb. Collier's 60:20, 25, December 29

1918

The reflection. Collier's 60:25, January 12; Same. Literary Digest 61:44, June 7, 1919

To a very young gentleman. Century 95:460, January; Same. Literary Digest 56:32, February 2; Same. Current Opinion 67: 55-56, July, 1919; Same. Weekly Review 5:207, September 3, 1921

Easter dress. Ladies' Home Journal 35:20, March

The prize package. Collier's 61:14-16, 32, March 23

Travels in Philadelphia. Philadelphia Evening Public Ledger, March 11, 1918 to January 27, 1920. The column appeared on the editorial page of the "Evening Ledger" for approximately two years. In addition to the column heading noted above, Morley used a number of other titles, including "The Chaffing Dish," "The Electric Chair," "Prunes and Prisms," "Elbow Room," and "Rubber Heels." The column was occasionally signed but more frequently appeared without signature or under the pseudonym Socrates. Morley's favorite topics in these sketches are books, streets, and food. Some of the earliest published writings of distinguished authors such as William McFee and Mrs. Etsu Inagaki Sugimoto appeared in his column. A selection of the sketches appeared in the book "Travels in Philadelphia," published in 1920.

The trees. Collier's 61:26, March 30

Engineer. Ladies' Home Journal 35:18, April

Woman who polished the apples. Ladies' Home Journal 35:20, April

Kitchener. Literary Digest 57:38, April 27

Lines for an eccentric's bookplate. Bookman 47:329, May

Eleven hours of moonlight. Ladies' Home Journal 35:16, June

Kathleen. Metropolitan Magazine 48:11-15, 60-61, 63-69, 71-72, June

From an office window. Ladies' Home Journal
35:12, August

Grace before writing. Bookman 47:611, August

On filling an ink-well. Bookman 47:609-611, August

To a grandmother. Collier's 59:20, August 18

Parnassus at home. Bookman 48:93-102, September (Chapter I of "The Haunted Bookshop"
with changes)

Christmas eve. House and Garden 34:16, December; Same. Primary Education-Popular Edu-
cator 46:270, December, 1928

English and American poets. Life 72:996, December 26
Reputed to be the work of Morley. The general
line of the article is to criticize the British for
knowing nothing of the rising American poets and
to throw off on Ezra Pound for having given
American poets a bad name.

1919

A meeting of the corn cob club. Bookman 48:534-43,
January (Chapter II of "The Haunted Bookshop")

The why of it. Publishers' Weekly 95:241, January
25

Titania arrives. Bookman 49:1-8, March (Chapter
III of "The Haunted Bookshop")

Charm. Mentor 7:11, April 1

Hallowe'en memory. Literary Digest 61:44, June 7

The haunted bookshop. Bookman 49:482-491, June (Chapter VI of "The Haunted Bookshop")

Hostages. Collier's 64:22, August 16

Sunny side of Grub Street. Bookman 50:10-13, September

In memoriam Francis Barton Gummere. Haverford College bulletin, 18, #2. Alumni quarterly pp. 29-35, October

To Louise. House and Garden 32:24, December

1920

The Bowling Green. New York Evening Post, February 9, 1920 to December 31, 1923 (Title varies: The Evening Post, February 9 to November 15, 1920)

The column appeared on the editorial page under the heading noted above and was signed, in print, by the author. It contained essays, poems, anecdotes, and epigrams by Morley; poems by other authors, such as John Crowe Ransom; and, with increasing frequency, letters to the columnist. Three of four books must be credited to the work that Morley contributed to the 'Post.' One of these was an anthology of verse contributed to the column and published under the same title in 1924. It included the contributions of such distinguished literary figures as Hilaire Belloc, Stephen V. Benet, William Rose Benet, Edna St. Vincent Millay, William McFee, and Elinor Wylie.

The colyumnist's confessional: II Christopher Morley by himself. Everybody's Magazine 42:29-30, February

Ballade of librolarceny. Weekly Review 3:252, September 22

William McFee—engineer and novelist. Publishers' Weekly 98:1189, October 16

Battle of manila envelopes. Bookman 52:227-233, November

Preface to the profession of journalism. Outlook 126:599-600, December 1

The perfect reader. Literary Review, December 24; Same. Golden Book Magazine 9:16, January, 1929

1921

The rudeness of poets. Literary Review, January 15

Keats (1821-1921). Bookman 52:553, February; Same. Current Opinion 70:552-553, April

Punch and Judy: A tale. Outlook 127:260-261, February 16

Curious case of Kenelm Digby. Bookman 53:10-20, March; 53:157-161, April

The autogenesis of a poet. Literary Review, April 30

In an auction room. Current Opinion 70:553, April; Same. Saturday Evening Post 199:126, April 23, 1927; Same. Bookman (London) 74:133, May, 1928

De senectute. Literary Review, May 28

Diarists. Weekly Review 4:599, June 25; Same. Literary Digest 70:34, July 16

Disappearance of Dunraven Bleak. Bookman 53: 312-321, June

Flight. Weekly Review 5:33, July 9

Inquest on a columnist. Literary Review, July 23

Only a matter of time. Atlantic Monthly 128:79, July

Vachel Lindsay. Bookman 53:525, August

Wind before breakfast. Weekly Review 5:207, September 3

At the mermaid cafeteria. Current Opinion 71:517, October

Poets in the cellar. Literary Review, October 22

Romeo and Juliet. Life 78:21, October 27

Protective coloring hastily self-applied by Christopher Morley upon being asked for an "autobiography." The Trend 1:5, November 7

Children as copy. Outlook 129:437, November 16

Christmas in the bookshops. Publishers' Weekly 100:1927, December 17

Mr. Pepys Christmas. Literary Review, December 24

Soliloquy for a third act. Atlantic Monthly 128:805-806, December; Same. Literary Digest 71:32, December 17

Worst Christmas story. Bookman 54:303-308, December

1922

Translations from the Chinese. Literary Review,
April 8

Continuity. Scribner's Magazine 71:753-758, June

Suitable honors for the unknown citizen. Literary
Digest 74:38-39, September 30

1923

Bedroom suite. Outlook 133:79-82, January 10

Rare books. Literary Review 3:393-395, January 20

Confessions of an amateur lecturer. Outlook 133:
179-181, January 24

The best books of the century. International Book
Review 1:5-7, May (Morley is one of ten contributors to this article)

So this is Arden. Literary Review 3:679, May 12

Of a child that had fever. Century 106:192, June

To a foreigner. Harper's Monthly Magazine
147:124, June

On a portrait of Dr. Johnson. Literary Review,
3:825, July 14; Same. Literary Digest 78:41,
August 4

Our house. Literary Digest 78:34, July 21

That one might almost say. Literary Review 3:
857-858, July 28

Tropes and tropics; parody on The tempest. Literary Review 3:895, August 11

Memoranda for a sonnet sequence. Harvard Graduates' Magazine 32:17-22, September

On the shelf. Literary Review 4:385-386, December 22

1924

Creative life. Yale Review (new series) 13:797-801, July

John Crowe Ransom. The Borzoi Broadside 3:34, July-August (A house organ published by Knopf. Morley's account deals with Ransom as a poet and reviews his "Chills and Fever.")

Religio journalistici. Century 108:331-344, July

The Bowling Green. Saturday Review of Literature August 2, 1924 to April 2, 1938.
In the decade following his "Post" engagement, Morley supplied the "Saturday Review" with "The Bowling Green" which contributed so greatly to that magazine's brilliance during this period. A critical anthology of Morley's writings would draw heavily on "The Bowling Green" which included much of the long series of light verse "Translations from the Chinese," the novel "Human Being," the familiar essay represented by "Streamlines," plays, and lectures. Morley continued as a "contributing editor" to the "Saturday Review of Literature" up to and including the March 29, 1941 issue.

Sea shell in Normandy. Saturday Review of Literature 1:7, August 2; Reprinted, Saturday Review of Literature 27:57, 60, August 5, 1944

East of Eden. New Republic 39:318-323, August 13

Memorandum for a subway station. Atlantic
Monthly 134:181, August

Walt; a one-act portrait. Bookman 59:646-662,
August

Slow gin. Saturday Review of Literature 1:339-340,
December 6

Points of view. A suggestion. Saturday Review of
Literature 1:388, December 13

1925

Baedeker fibbed. Harper's Monthly Magazine
150:176-187, January

A word about Joseph Conrad. Mentor 13:24-26,
March

Story of a white blackbird by Alfred de Musset;
translated by Christopher Morley. Golden Book
Magazine 1:499-510, April

Trade Winds. Saturday Review of Literature, July
4, 1925 to November 9, 1940.
Appeared irregularly under the pseudonym P.E.G.
Quercus. Anecdotes, commentary, and reminiscences about booksellers, publishers, readers,
books, food, and drink.

Thunder on the left. Harper's Monthly Magazine
151:390-412, September; 151:589-613, October;
151:699-721, November; 152:107-119, December

Tree that didn't get trimmed. Country Life (American) 49:33-34, December; Same. World Review
5:204-205, December 19, 1927

Arrow. Harper's Monthly Magazine 152:265-274, February; 152:445-456, March

Good theatre. Saturday Review of Literature 2:695-697, April 10; Same. Scholastic 25:7-9, October 13, 1934

Chateau de Missery. Saturday Review of Literature 3:17, August 7; Reprinted, Saturday Review of Literature 27:60, August 5, 1944

Paumanok. Saturday Review of Literature 3:363, December 4

Pleased to meet you. Harper's Monthly Magazine 154:7-20, December; 154:205-219, January, 1927; 154:375-382, February, 1927

1927

Calling on the trade. Publishers' Weekly 111:487-488, February 5

Invocation to an audience. Saturday Review of Literature 3:621, March 5; Reprinted, Saturday Review of Literature 27:60, August 5, 1944

The high, wide and handsome Transylvania. The Cunarder 11:17-19, April 11:27, May

Three trees. World Review 4:139, April 4

What lies beyond the grave. McCall's Magazine 54:10, 60, April

Christopher Morley writes about his trip on the "Champion" 20th century. New York Central Lines Magazine 8: 9-10, May

Curfew song. Delineator 111:5, October

Story of ginger cubes. St. Nicholas 54:746, October

Story of Louise's garden. St. Nicholas 54:946-947, October

Ferdinand and the taste for cheese. Forum 78:703-707, November

Pilot light. St. Nicholas 55:8-9, November

Unamiable child. Country life (American) 53:34-36, December

1928

Wooing song for Sir Toby. New Yorker 3:14, February 18

Song for a little house. Journal of the National Education Association 17;83, March

The sectarian broils on this poor planet. American Hebrew 49:769, April 6

A letter to Tom Daly. Commonweal 8:14-15, May 9

Really, my dear. Forum 79:723-735, May

Translations from the Chinese. Literary Digest 97:32, June 16

The peanut roaster. New Yorker 4:17, June 23

Essayage. New Yorker 4:14, July 21

Abandoned husbands. Saturday Review of Literature 5: 269-270, October 20

A Prolog for Rialto. New York Times, November 25
Tangled. Delineator 113:22, November

When Brady waves—it's 3:05! Collier's 82:24-25,
November 10

A fling at play-producing. Theatre 48:15-16,
December

The goldfish under the ice. McCall's Magazine
56:24-25, December; Reprinted, The Graphic
126:7-8, 66, 68, November 25, 1929.

Book-Of-The-Month Club News, 1928, et. seq.
Morley has been a member of the editorial board
since the inception of the Club. He is a frequent
contributor of book notes and reviews.

1929

Perfect reader. Golden Book Magazine 9:16,
January

She troupes to conquer. Literary Digest 100:30,
February 9

Three blind mice. Public Health Nurse 21:322,
June

Hoboken nights. Saturday Evening Post 202:14-15,
July 13

"S.O.B." Personally conducted tour of Hoboken
free state. Theatre Magazine 50:37, 58, October

It's a terrible thought. Life 94:11, November 1

John Mistletoe, '10. Haverfordian 49:45-51,
November

1930

Animal crackers; a poem. Childhood Education
6:256, February

Dogwood tree. Saturday Review of Literature
6:1158, June 28

Good deed. Collier's 86:28, August 23

He lays his finger on his nose. Collier's 87:38-39,
October 25

Time to light the furnace. Golden Book Magazine
12:40-41, November

1931

Ideal convention ground. Publishers' Weekly
119:2401, May 16

Club of abandoned husbands. Golden Book Magazine 14:48-50, August

On a change of style. Saturday Review of Literature 8:182, October 10

To a child. American Federationist 38:1268,
October

Old thoughts for Christmas. Golden Book Magazine
14:414-416, December

1932

To the little house. American Federationist 39:60,
January

Pebbles from Gissing pond. Atlantic Monthly
149:143-152, February

Two enthusiasms. Atlantic Monthly 149:403-406, April

John Mistletoe remembers Lindsay. Elementary English Review 9:128, May

Conrad and Stevenson; extract from Ex libris carissimis. Catholic World 135:472-3, July

On laziness. Golden Book Magazine 16:29-30, July

What the president reads. Saturday Review of Literature 9:117-120, September 24

Commutation chophouse. Golden Book Magazine 16:481-487, December

1933

World's most famous oration. Golden Book Magazine 18:102, August

Footnotes for a centennial, excerpt. Literary Digest 116:33, November 18

1934

Thirty out of forty-eight. American Traveler 2:5-7, 23-24, June

Signboard for an oasis; maladie du siècle; full and by. Scholastic 25:13, October 13

Eumenides of book collecting. Haverfordian 54:5-7, November

Origin of a clever quip. Ars Typographica 1:45, Autumn

1935

Christopher Morley writes an anniversary letter to
the book shops. Book Dial 12:10, (Christmas
issue, #4, Doubleday, Doran Book Shops).

A creed. World Digest 2:12, January

In re Logan Pearsall Smith. Haverfordian 54:69-
71, January

Prize awards for student libraries. Publishers'
Weekly 127:2138-2139, June 1

Old loopy . . . a love letter from Chicago. Inland
Topics (Chicago) 6:[18-21], November

The return of Huckleberry Finn. Columbia University Quarterly 27:370-378, December

1936

Home, suite home. Journal of Home Economics
28:36, January

Going through the Panama Canal. Scholastic 28:10,
12, April 4

Commencement address, June 15, 1936. Wheaton
Alumnae Quarterly 15:3-6, August (Morley's
remarks were taken down by a stenographer
since he made no use of notes.)

Too real to be fiction. Wings (Literary Guild,
N. Y.) 10:10-11, September

Books of the fall. Saturday Review of Literature
14:26, 28, October 10

1937

Bibliodisiacs. Saturday Review of Literature
15:sup. 7-8, March 27

Ballade of an old friend. New Yorker 13:27, May 22

Confessions of a pipe smoker. Pipe and Pouch (Pipe
and Tobacco Guild, Ltd. N. Y.) vol. 1, no. 1, p. 9

To Hilaire Belloc. Commonweal 26:40, May 7

Washing the dishes. Good Housekeeping 104:79, May

A successor to Mark Twain. Michigan Alumnus
Quarterly Review 43:602-616, July. 24

Literature through a knothole. Atlantic Monthly
160:182-188, August

Recuyell of the histories of Troy. Atlantic Monthly
160:458, October

Parnassus on wheels; a chapter from a novel for
bookworms. Scholastic (combined edition) 31:4-
6, 35, November 20

Why the Trojan horse was so written; letter to F. F.
Frazier. Saturday Review of Literature 17:16-17,
November 27

Dogwood berries. Book Dial 14:8-9, Christmas.
(Christmas issue, #4, of the Doubleday, Doran
Bookshops)

1938

Toulemonde: the golden germ. Saturday Review of
Literature 17:13-14, February 26; Excerpt, Saturday Review of Literature 26:28, September 18,
1943

Drug store. Coronet 3:3-5, March

To the editors of Cameo. Cameo (Knox College) no. 1, pp. 1, 16, April 8

Morley on maps. Time 31:5, May 2

Travels with a ghost. Saturday Review of Literature 18: 13-14, May 7

Translations from the Chinese. Saturday Review of Literature 18:12-13, May 21; 18:10, July 23; 19:13, November 5

Entrance to a wood. Saturday Review of Literature 18: 13-14, June 4

Long stories short. Saturday Review of Literature 18: 13-14, June 18

E. V. Lucas (1868-1938). Saturday Review of Literature 18:13, July 2

Marigold garden. Saturday Review of Literature 18:13-14, July 9

Discretion in midsummer. Saturday Review of Literature 18: 4, July 16

The folder. Saturday Review of Literature 18:11-12, August 20

Visiting fireman (I Main Line). Saturday Review of Literature 18:15-17, September 3

Visiting firemen (II Message on a Lump of Coal). Saturday Review of Literature 18:12, 16-17, September 10

Channel fever. Saturday Review of Literature 18: 12, 15, September 24

Ammonoosuc. Saturday Review of Literature 18:8, October 8

History of an autumn. Saturday Review of Literature 18: 18, 28, October 15

Map with a curly line. Saturday Review of Literature 19:12, November 19

Supper of larks. Saturday Review of Literature 19:13, 26, December 3

Exile. Saturday Review of Literature 19:13-14, December 17

Ampersands. Saturday Review of Literature 19:12-13, December 31

1939

Notes on Baker Street. Saturday Review of Literature 19: 12-14, January 28

To whom it may concern. Good Housekeeping 108:11, January

Mind raid precautions. Saturday Review of Literature 19:12, 14, March 4

Passivity program. Saturday Review of Literature 20:17, 20, 23, April 29 (Excerpts appear also in Everyday Reading 8:61-2, December 1-14, 1939)

Chevvy that hung her head. Scholastic 35:25E-26E, September 25

Endless river: Felix Riesenberg, 1879-1939, Saturday Review of Literature 21:17, 26, December 2

The bird that didn't go south; a four-minute story by Morley illustrated by Mortimer Wilson. This Week Magazine (New York Herald Tribune) pp. 8, 12, December 3

Christmas stocking; or, poor man's gout. Saturday Review of Literature 21:13-14, December 16

Heywood. Saturday Review of Literature 21:8, December 30

1940

Up the hill. Scholastic 36:13-14, April 22

Broken English. Good Housekeeping 110:66, May; Same. Saturday Review of Literature 23:9-10, December 7

Fluctuat nec mergitur. New York Times Magazine p. 15, June 23

Radio that went on talking. Atlantic Monthly 165:844-846, June

Specialty shopping. Good Housekeeping 110:70, June

Conversation by mail by Christopher Morley, Franklin P. Adams, Margaret Fishback, and Henry Morton Robinson. Reader's Digest 37:1-5, July

Mrs. Forsooth. Good Housekeeping 111:64, July

Letters from a young man. Good Housekeeping 111:118, August

Hampstead coach, February 3, 1820. Stack (Haverford College) 2:4, Autumn

Kitty Foyle. Philadelphia Evening Bulletin, December 9-20 (Appeared daily except December 15, 22, 25, and 29)

Sonnet with an allergy. New Yorker 16:119, December 14

1941

Literature from above. Saturday Review of Literature 23:10, January 11

Shakespeare and ivory bomb shelters. Saturday Review of Literature 24:3-4, 17, April 26

Kitty Foyle's creator greets us Greggites. Gregg Writer 43:491-92, June

The archway. Haverford Review 1:10-11, Autumn

1942

Only the wise would guess. Saturday Review of Literature 25:7, June 13

Proprietor. Atlantic Monthly 170:61, July

Letter to a publisher on Max Beerbohm's birthday. Saturday Review of Literature 25:8-9, October 24

Letters more or less personal. College English Association. News Letter 4:2, October, 1942 (Letter from Morley explaining that the hero of his novel "Thoroughfare" is the English language.)

Ballade in a bookseller's catalogue. New Yorker
19:60, February 27

The Barton autograph book. Haverford Review 2:
28-29, Spring

Tablet for some ruins. Saturday Review of Literature 26:11, November 6

Christopher Morley, "Inaugural Address." Library
Associates of Haverford College, Bulletin, no. 1,
pp. 3-4, November 20 (mim.).

Around the clock, New York Post, Weekly Picture
Magazine section p. [7], December 4 (Excerpts in
Saturday Review of Literature 26:20, December
18)

1944

Dear pleasures. Pleasures of Publishing 11: [1],
March 20 (A letter to the Editor of "Pleasures
of Publishing" from Christopher Morley.)

Toulemonde: intermezzo. Saturday Review of Literature 27:15, April 29

Old mandarin. Atlantic Monthly 174:103, 105, July;
174:110, 113, September; 174:114, 117, November;
175:124, March, 1945; 175:121, 123, May, 1945;
175:120, June, 1945; 176:121, September, 1945

Bowling green. [Weeding beets] Saturday Review of
Literature 27:56-57, August 5 (Special contribution to the "Saturday Review of Literature" on
the occasion of its 20th anniversary. The "Bowling Green" column was discontinued April 2,
1938)

Requiesco on Riverside. American Mercury 59: 208-209, August

What happened at Quebec. Saturday Review of Literature 27:5-6, 29-31, September 30

1945

Another letter to Lord Chesterfield from Sam Johnson. Saturday Review of Literature 28:14, February 10

Triumph of the egg. Saturday Review of Literature 28:12, March 31

Nie wieder. New York Times Magazine p. 20, April 22

Ballade of the welkin. Saturday Review of Literature 28:8, May 26

Momentum. Commonweal 42:281, July 6

Last word. Saturday Review of Literature 28:21, September 1

Laws of war. Commonweal 42-569, September 28

Outline of history. New Yorker 21:57, September 29

Ballad of New York, New York. American Mercury 61:446-447, October

Sheep meadow. Saturday Review of Literature 28:44, November 3

Translations from the Chinese. New York Times Magazine p. 12, November 11; p. 61, February 10, 1946; p. 4, April 28, 1946; Saturday Review of Literature 32:54-55, August 6, 1949

Codeine (7 per cent). Ellery Queen's Mystery
Magazine 6:42-45, November

Sheep meadow speech. Commonweal 43:110-112,
November 16

Byron and water. Saturday Review of Literature
28:37, November 24

1946

Chill, no coat. Saturday Review of Literature 29:
10, January 19

Clinical Notes By A Resident Patient. The Baker
Street Journal, January, 1946, et seq.
Commentary and reminiscences about Sherlock
Holmes.

Watson a la mode. Baker Street Journal 1:15-20,
January. (Written under the pseudonym Jane
Nightwork.)

What is civilization? Ladies' Home Journal 63:23,
January

Mercy stroke. Saturday Review of Literature 29:
14, February 2

Ram's horn. Commonweal. 43:428, February 8

Poems on postcards. Commonweal 43:500, March
1; 43:600, April 5; 44:138, May 24; 44:237, June
21

Overstate of the union; My mind to me a kingdom
is. Commonweal 43:548, March 15

Saguenay; Three-star, would I were steadfast. Saturday Review of Literature 29:59, March 23

Big three. Saturday Review of Literature 29:24,
May 4

The Consolable Widow. Ellery Queen's Mystery
Magazine 7:40-53, May

Operation equator; Chinese fable. New York
Times Magazine p. 44, May 26

Child's atoll of verses. Saturday Review of Literature 29:12, July 6

From an airplane. Saturday Review of Literature
29:20, December 21

1947

Private enterprise. Atlantic Monthly 179:67,
January

Robert C. Holliday. New York Herald Tribune
Section II, p. 7, January 12

Bronzino's mixture. Saturday Review of Literature 30:13-14, 67, April 12

Cockrow in spring. Saturday Review of Literature
30:20, May 3

Time of life. '47 Magazine of the Year 1:88-89,
June

Dove Dulcet hitches his wagon. Ellery Queen's
Mystery Magazine 10: 111-113, July

American gentleman. Saturday Review of Literature 30:16-17, September 20

Musings from "The Old Mandarin." Courier
(London) 9:141-143, October

St. Bypass-under-the-bridge; When civilization
came to wending ways, a story. '47 Magazine of
the year 1:21-28, December

Sherlock Holmes revisits Cambridge. Courier
(London) 9:87-89, December

1948

A letter from Christopher Morley. Haverford
Quarto pp. 1-3, Spring (Letter dated Roslyn
Heights, N. Y., January 26, 1948, to Henry G.
Rickerman, Editor of "The Quarto.")

Letters to the editors. Life 24:13, March 1 (A
letter from Christopher Morley, n.d., comment-
ing on his brother's endorsement of Senator
Taft for president.)

Thoughts on not being able to attend the annual
meeting of the College English association. Saturday Review of Literature 31:34, March 27

Notes on an island. I. General Inference. Saturday
Review of Literature 31:11-14, 58-59, April 17

Notes on an island. 2. L for learner. Saturday
Review of Literature 31:8-9, 37-40, April 24

[Excerpt] from "Lord of Semitones." Saturday
Review of Literature 31:39, May 1 (Appeared in
"The Phoenix Nest")

From Christopher Morley. Word Study 24:6,
October, 1948 (A letter from Morley explaining
the term "kinsprit" which he coined.)

Brief case, or, every man his own Bartlett. Saturday Review of Literature 31:20, November 6

Thomas Augustine Daly. Philadelphia Inquirer,
"Books Section" p. 8, December 5

1949

Foggy Bottom. London Mystery Magazine 1:17-22
(no month given)

Roderick Usher's allergy. Saturday Review of
Literature 32:30, April 16

Nelson Doubleday. Saturday Review of Literature
32:22-23, March 5 (Letter to the editor on death
of Nelson Doubleday)

My tables . . . set it down. Saturday Review of
Literature 32:7, May 7

On belonging to clubs. New Colophon, a book collectors' quarterly 2:113-19, June

Translations from the Chinese. Saturday Review
of Literature 32:54-55, August 6

A new estimate of a great novelist. New York
Times Book Review p. 1, 15, August 14

To quote Mr. Morley; excerpts from Man who
made friends with himself. Reader's Digest
55:18, September

Report from Baker Street. New York Times Book
Review p. 45, November 27

Of an ancient spaniel in her fifteenth year. Atlantic Monthly 184:47, November

To a gentleman at Wayne University ("Letters to
the Editor"). Saturday Review of Literature
32:22, December 17

1950

Grandpa sings to himself. Atlantic Monthly
187:71, March

Epitaph for love. Saturday Review of Literature
33:48, March 11

Two soliloquies. Saturday Review of Literature
33:29, March 11

Honorable world. New York Times Magazine p.
20, March 19

Atomic fission, April 1387. Atlantic Monthly
185:94, April

Children's crusade. Saturday Review of Literature 33:16-17, April 15

In a second-hand bookshop. Antiquarian Bookman
5:1433, May 13

To his twilight reader [by Dove Dulcet]. Saturday
Review of Literature 33:56, May 13

Ballade of William Rose Benét. Saturday Review
of Literature 33:11, May 20

"Heaven had no wall." Saturday Review of Literature 33:10-11, May 20 (Letter on the death of
William Rose Benét)

1950

Anthem for Boeotia. Harper's 201:87, September

Hickory and honeysuckle. American Mercury
71:366, September

From the Chinese. New York Times Magazine p. 44, September 10

Old mandarin at the U. N. New York Times Magazine p. 34, September 17

Interruptions (an essay in verse). American Mercury 71:464-50, October

Old farmer's almanac. Atlantic Monthly 186:95, October

The Boswell papers, a legend of impropriety. Saturday Review of Literature 33:11-14, 60-63, October 7

Sonnet on copyright (for Melville Cane). Saturday Review of Literature 33:26, October 28

To the Editor: [Letter of Christopher Morley explaining the term "hat trick" in "Letters to the Editor" column] New York Times Book Review p. 22, December 10

1951

Birdmaster general. Good Housekeeping 132:248, March

Thoughts in an Easter pew. Saturday Review of Literature 34:22, March 24

Good housekeeping. Good Housekeeping 132:147, April

Translations from somethingorother. Saturday Review of Literature 34:39, July 21

Hampshire autumn. Spectator 187:428, October 5

The new housemaid. Spectator 187:866, December
21

1952

Lucky dip. Saturday Review 35:18-19, 31, January
12

Poems. Atlantic Monthly 189:90, March

Gentlemen's relish. Saturday Review of Literature 35:12, March 15

Secrets of the library. Atlantic Monthly 189:89,
May

Hutch. Saturday Review of Literature 35:16,
June 21

Chain reading—happy sequences of reading you
don't have to do. New York Herald Tribune
Book Review 28:2, July 6

Middlewestern primary. Saturday Review of Literature 35:18, August 23

Prayer for the homestretch. Good Housekeeping
135:208, September

The old mandarin: flying saucers; more thoughts
about daddy Wordsworth. Saturday Review of
Literature 35:32, September 6

VI. PERIODICAL ARTICLES ABOUT
CHRISTOPHER MORLEY

The Rhodes scholarships. College Weekly (Haverford) 1:1, January 24, 1910
Biographical notes with pictures.

Quicksall, H. P. Sketch. Book News Monthly 36:205, February, 1918

O'Sullivan, Vincent. America and the English literary tradition. Living Age 303:170-176, October 18, 1919; Same, condensed. Literary Digest 63:27-28, October 18, 1919. The article appeared first in the New Witness (London) September 12, 1919, pages 410-413 under title above.

C.D.A. Jr. Tales from a rolltop desk. Haverfordian 41:79-80, November, 1921
Critical material in addition to notes on Morley's book of the same title.

Atkinson, J. Brooks. Bourgeois life in an optimist's mirror. Independent 108:49, January 21, 1922

MacIntosh, A. Christopher Morley's latest books. Haverfordian 41:158-162, February, 1922

Johnson, Merle D. and Hopkins, F. M. eds. American first editions, a series of bibliographic checklists; No. 35 Christopher Morley, compiled by Aaron Mendoza. Publishers' Weekly 103:1705-1706, June 2, 1923

Van Doren, Carl. Day in and day out: Adams, Morley, Marquis, and Brown, Manhattan wits. Century 107:308-315, December, 1923

The religion of a newspaperman. Literary Digest 80:31, January 19, 1924

Overton, Grant. An author you should know and why. Mentor 14:48-49, May, 1926

Christopher Morley: A biographical sketch. World Review 4:232-3, May 23, 1927

Pray for Ben Jonson? Literary Digest 94:24-25, August 20, 1927

Canby, Henry S. Christopher Morley. Saturday Review of Literature 4:625-626, February 25, 1928

Matthews, T. S. Christopher Morley. New Republic 54: 167-169, March 21, 1928

Lee, Harriet H. Drama in the last seacoast of Bohemia; Rialto theatre, Hoboken, N. J. (illustrations). Drama Magazine 19:140-141, February, 1929

Moses, Montrose J. How New York was sent to Hoboken. Review of Reviews 79:134-136, May, 1929

Goodman, N. G. Christopher Morley puts Hoboken on the map. General Magazine and Historical Chronicle 31:451-454, July, 1929

Canby, Henry S. Christopher Morley. English Journal (High School ed. and College ed.) 19:9-11, January, 1930

McCord, David. Christopher Morley. English Journal (High School ed. and College ed.) 19:1-9, January, 1930

L.A. and F.W.L. To C.M. Haverfordian 50:476-477, January, 1931

Hopkins, Frederick M. Appointed a Rosenbach
lecture fellow in bibliography, University of
Pennsylvania. Publishers' Weekly 119:2527-
2528, May 23, 1931

Brindze, Ruth. Read some "worst sellers" for a
change; an interview with Christopher Morley.
Enlightened Homes 3:4-5, 7, November, 1931

Barnes, George E. compiler. Bibliography,
American Rhodes Scholars. The American
Oxonian 19:1-159, January, 1932

Stone, Wilbur M. My Christopher Morley's.
American Book Collector 3:33-37, January,
1933

Song, Arthur. Where the blue begins. Hawaii quill
magazine 6:16-17, March 9, 1933
Critical essay on Morley's writings.

Poet philosopher of the home. Journal of Home
Economics 28:36, January, 1936

Selsor, Jackson. Notes for a Morley collector.
Book Collector's Journal (Chicago) 1:3, March,
1936

Miller, Mary I. Successful Christopher Morley.
Everyday Reading 8:63, December 1-14, 1936

Dullnig, Catherine. The Old Mandarin's disciple
consults the dictionary. Word Study Suggestion
leaflet (Merriam Company) vol. 1 #4, February,
1938. (Four unnumbered pages.)

Hamilton, Schuyler. Christopher Morley, the
original kinsprit. Avocations 1:550-559, March,
1938

Kunitz, Stanley J. Words on Morley. Wilson Library Bulletin 14:574, April, 1940

Burton, K. Why Kitty Foyle? Sign 19:752, July, 1940

Altick, Richard D. Average citizen in Grub Street: Christopher Morley after twenty-five years. South Atlantic Quarterly 41:18-31, January, 1942

Foley, Louis. "Fluctuat nec mergitur" suggested by Morley's sonnet; with text of sonnet. South Atlantic Quarterly 43:160, April, 1944

Gordon, Milton M. Kitty Foyle and the concept of class as culture. American Journal of Sociology 53:210-217, November, 1947

Lyle, Guy R. Toward a bibliography of Christopher Morley. Louisiana Library Association Bulletin 12:82-85, March, 1949

Breit, Harvey. Talk with Christopher Morley. New York Times Book Review. p. 13, July 31, 1949

Overton, Grant. Morleyiana. Hobbies 54:142, 153, August, 1949

VII. INDEX

A. Separates

Adams, Franklin P. —See Innocent Merriment.
Adams, J. Donald. —See Treasure Chest.
Adelphi College. —See Open Letter From Christopher Morley; Passivity Program.
Adler, Elmer. —See Breaking Into Print.
Adventure Of The Blue Carbuncle. —See Adventures Of Sherlock Holmes.
Adventures Of Hajji Baba Of Ispahan (Morier), 103.
Adventures Of Sherlock Holmes, The Adventures Of The Blue Carbuncle, 124; deluxe ed. 124.
Adventures Of Tom Sawyer (Twain), 93.
"All Quiet On The Western Front" (Remarque), 71.
Amenities Of Book-Collecting. — See Christopher Morley On The Amenities Of Book-Collecting.
American Essays (Shaw), 123.
American Estimates (Canby), 131.
American First Editions (Johnson), 131; 4th ed. (Blanck), 135.
American Nights Entertainment (Overton), 131.
American Novelists Of Today (Warfel), 137.
American Rhodes Scholars (Classbook), 89.
American Youth Hostels. —See AYH Handbook · 1941.
America's 93 Greatest Living Authors (Burnett), 116.
America's Town Meeting Of The Air. —See National Forum For The Discussion Of Public Questions.
Another Letter To Lord Chesterfield, 58; limited ed., signed, 59.
Anthology Of Children's Literature (Johnson), 123.
Anthology Of Light Verse (Kronenberger), 97.
Anthology Of Magazine Verse For 1935 (Pater), 100; For

1937, 106.
Apologia Of The Ampersand, 20. See also Diggings From Many Ampersandhogs.
Apologia Pro Sua Preoccupatione, 14.
Apology, An Explanation, And An Appeal (Abramson) 71.
Apology For Boccaccio, 9; large-paper ed., 9.
Appreciation Of Thunder On The Left (Walpole), 71.
Argus Book Fair, 71.
Arrival Of Wilhelm, 71.
Arrow, 11.
Atom Splitter. —See To Doctor R.
Author To The Printer, 71.
Autographing, 72.
AYH Handbook 1941, 114.
Babb, James T. —See Captain Macedoine Cocktail.
Back To Haverford And ----, 90.
Bacon, Francis. —See Essayes Or Counsels Civill & Morall.
Baker Street And Beyond (Smith), 111.
Baker Street Four-Wheeler (Smith), 118.
Baldwin, Charles C. —See Men Who Make Our Novels.
Ballade Of A. Horoscope. —See (Old) Farmer's Almanack.
Ballade Of An Old Friend. — See Geoffrey Chaucer (Rosenbach Company Catalogue).
Ballade Of The Day's Run, 72.
Barnacles From Many Bottoms (Typophiles), 97.
"Barns" —See Linweave Limited Editions.
Bartlett's Familiar Quotations, Eleventh Edition, 26; Twelfth Edition, 28.
Bastable Children (Nesbit), 92.
Beaumont, Francis (and Fletcher, John). —See Maides Tragedy.
Ben Abramson's Argus Book Shop Catalog 27, 72.
Benét, William Rose. —See Pocket University; Poems For Modern Youth; Poetry Package; Reviewing Ten Years.

181

183

Window, 75.
De La Mare.—See Tribute To
Walter De La Mare.
De La Roche, Mazo.—See Explorers Of The Dawn.
De Musset, Alfred.—See Two
Fables.
Designed For Reading, 95.
Devotion, 90.
Diamond, Henry R.—See Exhibition Wood And Linoleum
Engravings.
"Dibbies On It First."—See
Philip C. Duschnes Catalogue
29.
Dickinson, Asa Don.—See
Kaiser.
Diggings From Many Ampersandhogs (Typophiles), 102.
See also Apologia Of The
Ampersand.
Dilly Tante.—See Living
Authors.
Don Marquis Sons Of The Puritans (Marquis), 111.
Doubleday, Frank Nelson.—See
"Effendi."
Doyle, A. Conan.—See Adventures Of Sherlock Holmes;
Complete Sherlock Holmes;
Sherlock Holmes And Dr.
Watson.
Dreamthorp (Smith), 96.
Duschnes, Philip C.—See Catalogue 23; Philip C. Duschnes
Catalogue 29.
Dyer, Walter A.—See Story Of
A Belgian Dog.
Eat, Drink & Be Merry In Maryland (Stieff), 94.
Eaton, Anne Thaxter.—See
Poet's Craft.
Eddie Newton's Ride (Elkins), 75.
Eddy, Paul D.—See Open Letter
From Christopher Morley.
Editorial Room Broadside, 75.
Edson, C. L.—See Gentle Art
Of Columning.
"Effendi," 17.
Eighth Sin, 3; [Article About],
75. See also Breaking Into
Print.
"Eighth Sin On Parnassus."—
See Catalogue 23.
Elder, Donald.—See
Tolmanisms.
Elkins, William M.—See Eddie
Newton's Ride.

Elsea, Matilda Mahaffey.—See
Choice Poems For Elementary
Grades.
Emmett, Burton.—See Christopher Morley, His Books In
First Edition.
Encyclopaedia Britannica.—See
O. Henry.
England, Their England (Macdonell), 94.
Epigrams In A Cellar, 12. See
also New Yorker Book Of
Verse.
Equitable Trust Company Of
Atlantic City, 75.
Erskine, John.—See Contemporary War Poems.
Esoterica Viniana, 35.
"Essayage."—See New Yorker
Scrapbook.
Essayes Or Counsels Civill &
Morall Of Francis Bacon, 118.
Essays, 12.
Essays For Discussion (Forbes).
112.
Essays In Modern Thought
(Cook), 98.
Essays Of Yesterday And Today
(Lester), 118.
Essays Then And Now (Cooper),
104.
"Etiquette."—See Morrow's
Almanack For 1929.
Everett, Louella D.—See
Bartlett's Familiar Quotations; Cat In Verse.
Exhibition Wood And Linoleum
Engravings (Diamond), 75.
Ex Libris, 22; Fair edition, 23;
Lippincott edition, 23.
Ex Libris Carissimis, 16.
Explorers Of The Dawn (De La
Roche), 91.
Fair Warning.—See To The
Class of 1910.
Fallon, David.—See Essays
Then And Now.
Farma, William J.—See Prose,
Poetry And Drama For Oral
Interpretation.
Felix Riesenberg Living Again,
134.
Fifth Avenue Bus, 16.
50th Anniversary Columbia University Press Fall Books, 75.
Fles, Barthold.—See Best Short
Stories From Collier's.
Fletcher, John (and Beaumont,
Francis).—See Maides

184

187

188

Pater, Alan F.—See Anthology Of Magazine Verse For 1935; same, 1937.

Patriotic Pieces From The Great War, 80.

Patterson, Charles R.—See Some Ships Of Today And Yesterday.

Paumanok, 11.

"Peasant And King."—See Contemporary War Poems.

Peterson, Houston.—See Great Teachers; Poet To Poet.

Pharisees (Gibbon), 80.

Philip C. Duschnes Catalogue 29, 80.

Pictured Knowledge, 89.

Pipefuls, 7.

Pleased To Meet You, 12. See also Arrow.

Pleasures Of Smoking (Watkins), 125.

Pleasures Of Walking (Mitchell), 125.

Plum Pudding, 7.

Pocimur.—See Portraits And Self-Portraits.

Pocket Companion (Stern), 116.

Pocket University (Benét), 95.

Poems, 14.

Poems About God (Ransom), 81.

Poems For A Machine Age (McNeil), 115.

Poems For Modern Youth (Gillis), 108.

Poems Of Today (Cooper), 111.

Poetry Package, 65.

Poet's Craft (Daringer), 99.

Poet To Poet (Peterson), 120.

Porter, William Sydney.—See O. Henry.

Portraits And Self-Portraits (Schreiber), 133.

Portraits Of Thirty Authors (Jacobs), 134.

Posselt, Eric.—See World's Greatest Christmas Stories.

Post-Bag Diversions (Lucas), 96.

Pot Shots From Pegasus (Preston), 92.

Pottle, Frederick A.—See Boswell's London Journal.

Powder Of Sympathy, 9.

Preface To "Bartlett," 31.

Preston, Keith.—See Pot Shots From Pegasus.

Pride Of Sonnets, 66.

Principality And Power.—See New York World's Fair 1939.

Prize Awards For Student Libraries (McCawley), 97.

Profile By Gaslight (Smith), 119.

Prolegomenon To A Pack Of Sybilline Leaves From Argus.—See Blanket To Cover A Set Of Sheets.

Prologue For The Old Rialto Theatre, Hoboken, 14.

Proofreader's Mind, 81.

Prose, Poetry And Drama For Oral Interpretation (Farma), 102.

Rag-Picker Of Paris (Stirling), 32.

Ransom, John Crowe.—See Poems About God.

"Rare" Books, 19.

Rascoe, Burton.—See Morrow's Almanack For 1929; Smart Set Anthology.

Readers Digest Reader, 115.

Read, Warren W.—See Noble's Comparative Classics.

Really, My Dear . . . , 13.

Recitations Old And New For Boys And Girls (Gaige), 91.

Recognition Of Robert Frost (Thornton), 105.

Red Wine Of Youth (Stringer), 125.

Rehder, Jessie.—See Best College Verse, 1931.

Rehearsal, 10; association ed., 81. See also Treasury Of Plays For Women.

Religio Journalistici, 10.

Remarque, Erich Maria.—See All Quiet On The Western Front.

Return Of Huckleberry Finn.—See Mark Twain Commemoration.

Reviewing Ten Years (Benét), 132.

Ride In The Cab Of The Twentieth Century Limited, 13.

Riesenberg, Felix.—See Felix Riesenberg Living Again; Maiden Voyage; Riesenberg's "The Log Of The Sea"; Second Mate; Vignettes Of The Sea.

Riesenberg's "The Log Of The Sea," 81.

Rocking Horse, 3.

Rogers, Bruce.—See Barnacles From Many Bottoms; B R Marks & Remarks; B R's Secret Passion; [Number 25]

189

190

B. Articles

195